Listen to the Mourners

Listen
to the
Mourners

The Essential Poems of Nāzik Al-Malā'ika

NĀZIK AL-MALĀ'IKA

Edited and translated by 'Abdulwāḥid Lu'lu'a

UNIVERSITY OF NOTRE DAME PRESS
NOTRE DAME, INDIANA

University of Notre Dame Press
Notre Dame, Indiana 46556
undpress.nd.edu

Copyright © 2021 by the University of Notre Dame

Published in the United States of America

Library of Congress Control Number: 2021943169

ISBN: 978-0-268-20093-0 (Hardback)
ISBN: 978-0-268-20094-7 (Paperback)
ISBN: 978-0-268-20092-3 (WebPDF)
ISBN: 978-0-268-20095-4 (Epub)

CONTENTS

From *Sparks and Ashes* (1949)

From *The Wave's Nadir* (1957)

From *The Moon Tree* (1968) شجرة القمر

From *The Sea Alters Its Colors* (1974) يُغَيِّرُ أ لوانَه البحر

INTRODUCTION

Nāzik Al-Malā'ika (1923–2007)—viewed by any level-headed and un-biased literary critic—is the real pioneer of innovation in modern Iraqi and Arabic poetry. By "modern," I mean written in the middle years of the twentieth century, particularly those after the Second World War. In-novation in Arabic poetry began as early as the writing of the suspended odes of pre-Islamic Arabic poetry. Traditionally, a line of Arabic poetry should be self-sustaining, expressing a self-contained idea and a com-plete image within the line itself. An enlargement of that idea, or image, could be done in a second, third, or more lines, beginning those enlarge-ments with words like *and*, *or*, *but*, and the like, to show a second idea or a second image connected to what we found in the first line. One such example is found in the suspended ode of Al-A'asha (570–625) in the description of his sweetheart *Huraira* [little kitten!]. In line 12 of the poem, he says: "There is no luscious garden more aromatic, or better looking than she at the approach of sunset." But he says this in two lines rather than one, and the phrase "better than she" comes only in the third line. By pre-Islamic standards of poetry, this poetic device extended the meaning and description to three lines of poetry rather than one. And yet the image was so cleverly presented that we do not find a decent critical opinion with which to object to it. The example of innovation in the shape of the two-hemistiches line, so basic to traditional Arabic poetics, was "violated" by a certain *Umayyad*, an exceptional lunatic even for a poet, Deek-ul-Jinn of Ḥimṣ (777–849), who was so madly in love with his girl that he burned her, and out of her ashes he made a cup from which he drank and drank. . . . Yet we are not told what happened to him after that! What that extremely romantic poet wrote was a hemistich of three feet, and a second hemistich that had only two, while maintaining the same rhyme scheme throughout the poem. The poem is inordinately expressive of a man writhing on the fire of love, a rather absurd image even by present-day standards of exotic poetic expression.

In the 'Abbāsid period, with more and more non-Arabs permeating the predominantly Arab society, a rather quick and more than tangible development took place in the writing and singing of Arabic poetry. It was more than the mere introduction of non-Arabic words into the flourishing Arabic poetry under the 'Abbāsid caliphs; new forms of a poem, new Arabic words, and new, untraditional attitudes toward love poetry were introduced, developed, and, in many cases, adored. Abu-Nuwās presents a telling example in this respect:

> The wretched went looking for a ruin to ask,
> And I went looking for the town tavern.
> He cries about the departed of Asad tribe,
> Confound you: who are the Asadites?
> And who are the Tameemites and the like?
> The Arabs are nothing before God!

More detailed examples of development in Arabic poetry are found from Andalus between 711 and 1492, partially under the influence of the multilingual atmosphere in Muslim Spain, which, in turn, influenced the troubadour poetry of southern France and northern Spain, extending to Sicily and southern Italy and leading to the rise of a new lyrical poetry completely unlike Latin poetry in medieval Europe, which was mainly on ecclesiastical topics.

But the innovation in Arabic poetry, which Nāzik introduced, was not unaware of the steps in the development of Arabic poetry taken in the previous ages and in several Arab countries. She was a poet well versed in classical Arabic poetry and in prosody, and she was also very conscious of the withering state of Arabic poetry in her home country of Iraq, as well as in some other Arab countries. Growing up in a family that took culture and poetry seriously, she had assistance and guidance from her parents, both of whom were poets in their own right, and started developing her childhood poems by reading extensively on several aspects of poetry and literature in general. Nāzik published her first collection, *A Woman in Love with Night*, in 1947. That collection was expectedly highly romantic, in tune with the predominant Arabic poetry of the period, especially that of the Lebanese poets, and marked even more prominently by the Egyptian poets of the 1940s, who were not uncontaminated by the French attitudes of the turn of the century. Nāzik took a further distinct step in her second collection, *Sparks and Ashes*, published in 1949. This collection contained a poem titled "The Cholera," which was born, she says, on October 27, 1947, in which she expressed her shock at hearing news of the spread of that epidemic in Egypt. The form of the poem is completely different from that of the traditional two-hemistiches style of Arabic poetry predominant until that time, which Nāzik herself had observed in her poetry until then and her parents had preserved and revered. In the poem she varies the lengths of the lines and changes the rhyme scheme, according to the demands of the idea and the image, which could be expressed in a short line or in two, three, or four feet or more. Thus the first line of the poem has a measure of two feet only and is followed by a line of four feet, and so on, with a rhyme that changes with one, two, or more lines. Basically, the feet are the same as in Arabic prosody, but the arrangement is different now. She called that "free verse."

Here is the first section of "The Cholera," in translation:

The night calmed down.	2 feet – A
Listen to the fall of the sighs' echo,	4 feet – B
In the deep darkness, under the lull, on the dead.	6 feet – B
Cries arise, and tremble,	4 feet – C
Sadness pours, and flares,	4 feet – C
On it stumbles the sighs' echo.	4 feet – B
Rage is in every heart,	4 feet – D
Grief is in the quiet cottage.	4 feet – D
Everywhere there is a soul crying in the dark.	6 feet – B
Everywhere a voice rises.	5 feet – E
This is what death has torn,	5 feet – E
Death, death, death.	3 feet – E
O Nile! I am lacerated by what death has wrought.	7 feet – E

This is in the *mutadārak* (engendered) measure, the one added by al-Akhfash, al-Farāhīdi's pupil, to the original fifteen measures. It has four meters of *fa'lun*, strong/weak beats, in each of the two hemistiches as in the traditional form of Arabic poetry.

It is obvious that the poet has used the number of meters she has thought necessary for the idea or image in each line, varying the rhyme accordingly. In that sense, Nāzik's innovation in the arrangement of lines and meters was a major development in Arabic poetry-writing.

The first reaction to or rather rejection of that new arrangement came from the poet's own father, a staunch traditionalist who could not tolerate a disruption of the age-old metrical system, codified by Al-Khaleel Ibn Aḥmad Al-Farāhīdi of Baṣra (d. 786). But Nāzik's argument was that if an idea or image can be expressed in a line of two, three, or more feet, why should one stuff the line with sometimes unnecessary ideas or images only to adhere to the traditional measures in the two-hemistiches line of poetry? This sounds quite logical, but to call this "free verse" is simply saying the wrong thing for the right reason. The poet knew very well what the term "free verse" means, as it was coined by the American poet Walt Whitman in his *Leaves of Grass* in 1850. But the idea of freedom was celebrated in the mid-twentieth century in Iraq and other Arab countries. Therefore, I think, the poet wanted to use it for her newly developed form of the Arabic poem. The result was that many contemporary poets liked the idea and started writing in this new style, with various degrees of success, depending mostly on the poets' talent and mastery of traditional Arabic prosody. Among Nāzik's immediate contemporaries were outstanding poets like Badre Shakir Al-Sayyāb, 'Abdulwahhāb Al-Bayyāti, Buland Al-Ḥaidari, and others. This new development in the form of the poem led some of her contemporary poets to claim that they were pioneers in that form, and some of the contemporary literary commentators presented what were rather futile arguments as to who was the first to use this new form in writing poetry. But Nāzik continued writing in the new style, without abandoning the old style of two hemistiches and a monorhyme, though her poems were shorter and mostly in sections of six to eight lines, holding to the traditional measures but changing the rhyme with each new section of the poem.

The poet's argument was that lyrical poetry is more successful in the new style than in the traditional two-hemistiches style, which is more suitable for nonlyrical topics. She wrote extensively on the development of Arabic poetry, referring to her own experience, especially in her book *Problems of Contemporary Poetry*, published in 1962. But about that time, the poet seems to have been mindful of the numerous attacks on her experiments, so she sounded—to some critics at least—as if she had changed her mind about her "free verse" style. But, in fact, she pressed on, without abandoning the traditional form of poetry, all the way up until her latest iterations, especially in 1974, as we see in her collection *The Sea Alters Its Colors.*

Nāzik's argument about "free verse" was not easily accepted by serious critics, especially those who were well versed in European and American poetry. One such critic was my mentor, the late Jabra Ibrahim Jabra, who published a well-balanced criticism of the poet's argument titled "Free Verse and Wrong Criticism" (1949). Arguments about the name and concept of the new style followed, in periodicals and studies in Iraq and other Arab countries. I myself made some contributions to the argument, once in a public lecture in the "Cultural Season" of Kuwait University in 1968, titled "The Problem of Free Verse in Arabic Poetry," and again in another public lecture at the University of the United Arab Emirates in Al-Ain in 2010, titled "Free Verse and the Ongoing Mistake." I tried to show the obvious, that Walt Whitman's poetry had absolutely no rhyme or meter, whereas what Nāzik presented did have traditional Arabic meters and rhymes. I wondered on these occasions, and in my other writings, why Arab critics would not adopt the term "prose poetry" put forward by the Lebanese intellectual Ameen Al-Raiḥāni while he was in his self-imposed American exile, referring to Walt Whitman's poetry—as early as 1910!

A melancholic attitude toward life marks Nāzik's early poetry. She was an introverted poet, preoccupied with the duration of life and with inevitable death. She tells us in her introductions to her collections of poetry that she was under the influence of Schopenhauer, always wondering why people regard death as a bad thing when it is one way of putting an end to a bad life!

I have known Nāzik, first as a colleague in the College of Education at the University of Baghdad, formerly the École Normale Supérieure, her alma mater and mine, too, since 1957, and later as a teaching colleague at the University of Kuwait until 1970. I do not remember ever seeing the poet smile, let alone laugh, even though our Egyptian colleagues in Kuwait could not make more than a couple of statements without a joke somewhere along the line. In 1971–72, I spent a sabbatical year at Cambridge University doing research on troubadour poetry. About the beginning of the summer of that year, I received a letter from Nāzik, still in Kuwait, telling me that she would like to spend the summer in Cambridge and asking me to find a suitable apartment for her and her husband. I found a good self-catering apartment in a quiet area in Cambridge. When I went to the railway station to welcome the couple, I thought I would try a joke to see if I could force a smile from Nāzik. One of her poems was about utopia and says: "Utopia is a dream in my blood." So I greeted the poet by distorting the line into: "And England is a dream in my blood." Lo and behold, there appeared a bit of a smile, which soon disappeared under an oh-so-cloudy Cambridge summer. Some days later, my wife and I invited the couple to a luncheon in our house on Grantchester Road, and when the day arrived we wished to capture the occasion with a photograph on the large field opposite our house. There were six people in that picture, and when I held up my camera up, saying, "Ready?" in a second, Nāzik bent her head downward and closed her eyes. And so a rare occasion turned into yet another failure!

The poet was rather traditional in her clothes and behavior. She did not like makeup or any lavish clothes. A very close friend and neighbor, the late Dr. Ḥayāt Sharāra, our colleague in the College of Education, wrote a very good biography of the poet, providing very special and interesting information about her and her family. The book was published in January 1994. On the cover was a picture of a surprisingly happy-looking Nāzik, with a big smile and lips covered with bright- red lipstick. I think taking this photo must have been an act of sabotage on the part of the publisher, intended to shock people who had another image of the poet!

But Nāzik did have some moments of happiness, when a smile could have been detected on her face. Some of these rare moments she enjoyed when in 1948 she went, with some members of her family, on a trip to the northern mountains of Iraq, where she enjoyed the beautiful scenery of mountains and waterfalls in Sarsang. That natural, idyllic beauty suggested Utopia to her mind. She wrote a couple of poems on that and similar trips. Other rare occasions were when she was with children of her family or relatives, as she was very fond of children. She has such expression in a poem she wrote about her new-born child, Al-Barrāq. Other than on those rare occasions, the distinguishing characteristic of her poetry is various degrees of melancholy.

In 1971, two volumes of Nāzik's poetry came out from Beirut, Lebanon. The two volumes show the development of her poetry from the early 1940s up until 1971. But our poet never stopped writing poetry, in both the traditional and "free verse" styles. In 1974 a new collection titled *The Sea Alters Its Colors* came out from Baghdad. This collection shows a noticeable development in the style of her "free verse" and in the spirit of the poetry. We are told by Dr. Sharāra that the poet left some new poems unpublished. I wish I could get hold of those poems to see how they compare with the published poems of 1974.

The poet was very keen on expanding her knowledge of non-Arabic poetry and of modern languages, especially French, which was probably encouraged by her earlier steps in learning Latin. She had always wanted to study at a British or American university. Her wish was realized when in the summer of 1950 she won a Rockefeller scholarship to Princeton University. She spent a year there, but it was not a happy year emotionally because Princeton did not have women students in those days, and Nāzik found herself the only female at a university of young men. She never lost an opportunity to learn about poetry and criticism in the presence of eminent professors like Alan Tate, Richard Blackmore, Alan Downer, Donald Stouffer, and others. But the melancholy would not let go of her, mainly because she was so far away from her family and home atmosphere. Coming back to Baghdad in 1951, after the Princeton year, she started to write critical studies on poetry and literature in general. Most of her essays were published in Lebanese avant-garde periodicals. But the year 1953 was a particularly sad period for the poet, as her mother and some of her close relatives passed away, which was not helpful in altering the poet's melancholy disposition. Now she showed another interest, namely, writing about social and intellectual concerns, especially the position of women in her society. In September 1954, Nāzik won an Iraqi government scholarship to Madison, Wisconsin, to work for a master's degree in comparative literature. There she made friends with some of the women students, who were very encouraging and helpful, mostly wondering why a poet of such talent and culture needed to work for a university degree. Some of them told her that the professors did not feel at ease when they had such a highly talented and intelligent student in their lectures. Her classmates admired the lectures she was giving as part of her preparation for the degree. But this insinuation was realized, unfortunately, when the head of the English Department asked the poet to work for a BA in English literature, as she did not have one, but she had a first-class BA in Arabic. This did not discourage Nāzik; as she worked hard and managed to succeed in getting that BA before continuing her journey to the MA. During that time, the poet improved her knowledge of French to a degree that she could lecture and write an essay in French. On September 30, 1956, the poet returned to Baghdad with her degree in comparative literature, to be appointed to teach at her alma mater again. In June 1961, Nāzik was married to her colleague Dr. ‘Abdulhādi Maḥbooba, and a year later they had their first and only son, al-Barrāq, who would later obtain a PhD in literature.

The poet was a frequent visitor to Lebanon, and on one occasion, she found herself face to face with the celebrated Egyptian musician and singer ‘Abdulwahhāb, who was impressed by her musical and singing interests. She was celebrated on several occasions in Beirut, Damascus, and Cairo. In 1982 she resigned her job at Kuwait University and, in recognition of her contribution to poetry and teaching, the university gave her a one-year leave with full pay. She returned to Baghdad on February 15, 1987, and settled in a newly built house with her husband. In June 1992, the University of Baṣrah—where she had taught for several years, and where her husband had once been the president—conferred on her an honorary doctorate, although the University of Kuwait had been the first to do so.

On February 26, 1992, the family’s Toyota Super Saloon, which they had bought in Kuwait, was stolen. When Ṣaddām Ḥussein learned about this, he gifted her a brand-new Oldsmobile, on top of 1,000 dinars (US$3,300 at the time) given as a special retirement salary, in recognition of Nāzik’s contribution to Arabic poetry and culture.

A NOTE ABOUT
THE TRANSLATION OF
ARABIC POETRY

Every time I embark on the hazardous journey of translating Arabic po-
etry, I am haunted by a dictum of the celebrated medieval Arab literary
dictator Al-Jāḥiẓ (775–868) who said, "Poetry cannot be translated, and
it cannot be carried to another language, otherwise its metric system is
disrupted, its beauty is lost, and its admirable quality falls." This is par-
ticularly true with regard to the Arabic poetry of his time. Until recently,
the metric system and the monorhyme were basic to traditional Arabic
poetry. In our times, as much as in medieval times, traditional Arabic po-
etry presents formidable difficulties in translation. The Arabic language
has qualities not found in any European language, old or new. Declen-
sion of nouns, conjugation of verbs, and the dual number that affects
nouns, pronouns, adjectives, and verbs; the masculine and feminine signs
that affect nouns, pronouns, verbs, and adjectives in their singular, dual,
and plural forms cannot be handled in a modern European language, such
as English, French, Italian, Spanish, or German. A well-known line in
Arabic poetry describing two enchanting eyes of a damsel says: "Two
eyes which God ordered to be, and they did, acting to the minds what
wine acts." This is a pathetically lame translation because the imperative
"be" and the verbs "did" and "acting" are all in the dual in the original
Arabic. To use the plural instead of the dual fails to convey the beauty of

the line. In addition to that, we have adjectives in Arabic that could have two opposite meanings. The adjective *baṣīr* could mean "blind" or "able to see." The word *mawla* could mean "master" or "servant." The word "rain" has several synonyms in meaning, each different in form, each one denoting some difference in usage and nuance. Some creatures or animals have dozens of synonyms, no two of which mean exactly the same thing. The lion has dozens of names; so does the snake, the horse, the gazelle, and so on. These cannot be rendered in a non-Arabic language to mean, exactly, the same things they mean in Arabic or to suggest the same nuance. Moreover, names of certain characters, places, times, and historical incidents all have shades of meaning attached to them that cannot be conveyed into another language, and footnotes could be cumbersome and not very helpful. Certain turns of phrase in Arabic cannot be rendered in another language, which makes the translated version rather awkward and not "idiomatic" in the language of the translation. For all these reasons, one cannot help seeing the logic of our literary dictator of medieval times.

For this book I have chosen forty-one poems that I selected from six published collections by Nāzik. These are some of the poems that, I thought, could lend themselves rather easily to translation. I cannot say that I am quite satisfied with the results; I feel that there are points that could be further elaborated to suggest the shades of meaning that the poet intended.

For all these reasons, the translation of poetry, especially Arabic poetry, traditional and modern, must necessarily be a translation of meanings, with whatever conveyance of style and rhetorical images is possible. If stylistic precautions and pitfalls of any type were allowed to deter such translation, earlier translators would have been unable to translate into Arabic great works of literature such as the *Iliad*, the *Odyssey*, and works of similar, or even less important value, would have been out of reach for later generations.

Cambridge, May 2021
ʿAbdulwāḥid Luʾluʾa

From *Life Tragedy and a Song for Man*
(1945–1965)

مأساة الحياة وأغنية للإنسان

1. LIFE TRAGEDY

In vain you dream, my poetess,
There is no morn for this life's night.
In vain you ask, the secret will not clear,
You will not enjoy the undoing of bonds.

In the shade you spent your hours,
Perplexed, and by secrets anguished.
Asking the shades, and the shades nothing know,
But the destinies do know.

Forever at the unknown horizon you stare,
Perplexed; but has the hidden cleared?
Forever you ask, but the sneering destiny
Is an eternal and obdurate silence.

Why don't you despair? No heart has yet
Realized the secrets; so how can you hope to realize?
Sorry, my girl, you will not understand
Times. So be content to ignore them.

Leave the weary barque to the hands of destiny,
To steer it the way they like.
What have you gained from wrestling with the waves?
Has misery winked away from your hopes?

O, you whose life was lost in dreams!
What have you gained but boredom?
Its secret is buried still;
What waste of life you spent in queries!

It is the secret of life, too abstruse to conceive
By men of wisdom, with which they could not cope.
So despair, my girl, its secrets were not conceived
Before; so whence is hope?

Before you came to life, millions had come,
Then they disappeared and perished.
I wonder what they have gained
Of their nights! Where are the festivals and feasts?

Nothing of them remained, except sorrowful graves,
Laid on the banks of life.
They left the precincts of being,
And sought the world of death.

How long has gloomy night covered the spheres,
And how long to it the worlds have succumbed?
The night proved that it has been as before,
But where are those who yesterday were?

How, O Time, between your hands, the hopes die out,
And the dreams their fervor lose?
How do hearts wither when they are so bright?
And darkness live, though it is dark?

How can thorns live on, but pleasant blooms
Decay, in the grip of storms?
How can chants in perdition fall,
But remains the mockery of fate?

Talk to the heart, you, tragedy,
You who were called life!
What will you do with me in the unknown future?
What will happen to my remains?

What grave have you prepared for me,
A cave immersed in darkness,
Or will my barque drown with me one day,
So I will settle under dark waves?

O life, how I am tossed about by delusions,
How fatigued by thoughts!

Constantly I ask the night about death,
And what the lot will be.

How often I have asked my night,
But the answer is rare in this life.
There is nothing but illusions, mocking me,
Nothing but dreams mixed with confusion.

Have I understood enough of life
To understand death and come nearer to its secret?
The world of death is still an enigma,
Too much for my weary heart to solve.

Well, life! I shall not ask the night
About the secret, so judge the way you like.
Give me the life of flowers, I shall not cry,
Or extend my days, if you wish.

What use is weeping, when the heart of destiny
Does not listen to the criers!
Weeping will not add one day to my lifetime,
And death will not pity my misery.

Let life force me to swallow cups
Of grief and despair, the way her whims go.
Will death listen to my pleading?
If I hoped for its silence and peace?

This is the way I came to life, not knowing
Which way life would take.
I should live the way the unknown likes:
Perplexed, tossed about by dark spheres.

If I wanted to live, death would not listen,
Nor would it extend my years.
Or if I wanted to die, my hopes would not be heeded,
Nor would I meet my end.

This is what inevitable destiny wants,
Not what my hopes desire.
Life has steered me; I wonder
Where my vessel would anchor, by which sands?

Here am I: confusion and stupor,
Between a withered and a waning age.
I do not know the aim of my course,
Ah! I wish a secret would clear before my eyes.

Oh, shores of joy! I wish I could
Understand something about your unknown horizon.
I can no longer check my desire.
When, O shores, is my arrival?

Everything around me tells me about you,
But when is my meeting going to be?
Have mercy on me before the waves
Spoil my sail and the meteors rage.

Oh, shores of happiness! What are you?
An illusion, or a witnessed reality?
Would my stabbed heart ever reach you,
 Or are you a distant dream?

How often they have told my heart
About meeting you! But you are still a child's dream.
I am still spending my nights in weeping
And singing the sorrows of miserable existence.

My seat on my sand hill is still
Listening to my previous songs.
I am still a child, but I have become
More ignorant of my essence and lifetime.

(*Life Tragedy*, Beirut, 1970, pp. 21–30; *Complete Works*, vol. 1, 1971, pp. 21–30)

2. PAINS OF OLD AGE

Oh, pains of the old in the land, could you ever
    Dry in the miserable eyes!
Which old man does not shed warm tears,
    On what has passed, and complain about misfortune?

He is that grief stricken, who spent his youth
    In the flame of cares and sorrows.
Then he tasted youth, in a cup of tears,
    No hand its dust can remove.

Then youth disappeared in lifetime darkness,
    Loved ones and the supporters died.
Every year, he finds the loved ones perish,
    Their memory he faced by destiny.

What a caravan driven by deceptive destiny,
    Under winds and darkness!
Casting in the mouths of death
    One of its members, every morn and eve.

O, winter of life, there is no one left
    In this darkness, except this cheated wretch.
They were all, but him, taken by death,
    So his grieved moaning boomed.

It is that wretch, weakened by age,
    With ailments infecting his body,
Life darkness took away his light,
    And objects vanished from his grasp.

He knows that death is near to him,
    As near as sorrows and pains.
Every day he can almost sing the world,
    And lifetime, the farewell song.

(*Complete Works*, 1971, pp. 225–227; orig. pub. 1950)

3. IN SEARCH OF HAPPINESS

We searched for happiness, but
    We could not find its enchanted hut.
For ever we ask the nights about her,
    But she is the world's secret, and Time's riddle.

How long they have told my heart about her,
    In the nights of my childhood and youth.
How long they have portrayed her meeting my eyes,
    And cast news in my visions.

Sometimes she is nothing but perfume and colors,
    And songs and lights.
She does not live except at the door of a palace,
    Raised by hands of wealth and plenty.

Sometimes it is in abstention from worldly pleasures,
    And among ascetics and monks.
She does not live except on temple rocks,
    Between prayer and faith.

She is sometimes in sin, and base pleasures,
    In evil, harm, and dispute.
She cannot respond except to a base heart,
    Involved in evils and sins.

To some people, she lives with a shepherd,
    Who spends his life on lowlands and hills!
He sings with his flock, if he so likes,
    And dozes under fragrance and shades.

To others, she is the daughter of seclusion,
    Art, and sublime beauty.
Who cannot live except on a warbler's mouth,
    Who sings, or on the lips of a born poet.

Sometimes she is found in Love,
    Inspired by Cupid in every lover's heart.
She does not live except on a lover's lip,
    Singing his life a love tune.

They have told me about her so much,
    But I could not find her after long search.
I have spent the nights in search,
    Singing with it the beautiful world.

My lifetime has passed in vain, and I am still
    Walking on these grievous shores.
I found nothing in the sand except
    Remains of storms, what a cheated hope!

(*Song for Man*, 1970, pp. 397–404; *Complete Works*, vol. 1, 1971, pp. 66–69)

From *A Woman in Love with Night*
(1947)

عاشقة الليل

4. BURNT LIFE

The poetess wrote this poem when she threw her memoirs into the fire.

These, O fire, are my joys, desires, and sorrows.
I came to throw them between your jaws in my sorrowful dawn.
Whatever misery or desire have passed through my heart
Grab now, leave nothing, and do not wait for me.

These lines have included the remains of my years,
Since destinies cast me into the maze of life.
A child I was looking at the shore with tearful looks,
Seeing the world as a sea sunk in darkness.

All my years, O fire, were in these lines,
My songs, life desires, and my joy,

The remains of my yearning, splinters of my feeling,
 Tatters of dreams, and bitter sorrow.

They are, O fire, the flowers of my youth.
I forged them as a memory of my sorrows, a symbol of my torture.
Their lines were erased by my tears; wearied by my gloom,
So, take and turn them into a heap of dust.

Burn them, I no longer care, I will not miss their fragrance.
Those were, O fire, a memory of nights I shall not see.
The past has buried their secrets, and fully effaced them.
The forgetful wave has folded them in its deep night.

Those nights were gone, and Time has folded my youth.
What use is left, O fire, of my tears and sorrows?
What meaning is there of my remembrance, desires, and hopes?
The past will not return, my eyes will not see its glamour.

O Present, do not hasten the distant past,
Let the sun-carriage halt on the wide horizon,
Let our youth remain under the shades of eternity.
Ah! Let the word "past" be effaced from the book of life.

Or wipe out what sorrows the past has left in us,
Efface memory, and do not leave deep desire for us;
We have enough of the present pains, tears, and sorrows.
For pity, efface the past and the tearful years.

Why should my memoirs stay alive after me and I am forgotten?
Every day I walk away from the world in despair,
But they stay fresh and youthful in body and soul.
Oh, how violent and cruel is my hatred of remembrance!

O fire! Rage in the horrible withering fireplace,
And take from the charm of remembrance food for the flames.
Take revenge on it, melt it and turn it into ashes,
But let me once laugh from my dejected heart.

(*Complete Works*, 1971, vol. 1, pp. 486–489)

5. TRAVEL

Alone I am on the sea waves, O boat, return.
In vain is waiting, my star will not come out.
The wind blew on the fearful, mad sea.
So, return to the quiet shore with my bleeding heart.

Return to the shore, go back, I no longer like to stay.
The sea took my friends away to where there is light.
Alone I am, O mariner, sorrow and tears.
The boat returns with me alone when the evening comes.

They went to the enchanted shore, as I returned alone,
They went, except me, as I returned with my sorrow.
I gained nothing in my trip, except my yearning and fatigue.
So, O sea, let this be the last of my hopes.

How, O sea, has the caravan disappeared behind the island?
How does the dream of travel wither in my enamored heart?
Your waves, O sea, could not heal the departure pain.
So let me return, there is no pity now in the destiny heart.

Let me return to the dark shore, a frightened heart,
Burying my dreams, and living like a flower in the desert,
Forever watering my chants with the sorrows of the perplexed,
Forever dreaming of the dawn but finding no day.

O boat! Return with me, there is no longer a dream;
The caravan is gone, and no star will shine on my horizon.
What do I hope for, when around me is the evening,
And storms, and night phantoms, and sea?

O shore! O spring of my dreams! Farewell!
The oar is bored with my hands pushing and struggling.
How can I meet you when the wind has torn my sail?
And my hope in you among the waves, o shore, is lost.

Let me return, there is no travel today to the fair horizon.
I shall not see the shore, shall not dream under the palm shades.
Tomorrow is my major journey to the sunset valley.
Ah! Let me journey to it. It is time to go.
So farewell caravan and sorrows be turned off by death.
It is time for the tunes to quit my guitar and lute.
So welcome, O death! Welcome, O remains!

(*Complete Works*, vol. 1, 1971, pp. 513–516, July 30, 1945)

6. WHIPS AND ECHOES

"On the wet street floor, there was a body of a horse.
The whips were rising, then not falling except on a wound."

I still remember everything of my lost morning:
The wounded, bloodied, lying on the street floor,
And the echo of the wearying whips on the imploring forehead.

O revolt of feelings in my soul, why is my fearing?
My pain for the torn body is part of my foolish weakness.
Tomorrow I shall bury what is left of my tiring sympathy.

I wish I were blind, unaware of what evils commit,
Death, not hearing the fall of whips on the backs.
I wish my heart were a rock, not tortured my feelings.

I wish, what use is to you, my life, I wish?
Your blooming dreams have turned grievous despair.
The destructive destiny will not hear, so shout or succumb.

O fire of my gentle feelings, O strange among humans!
The fall of whips, on the backs, is more severe than destiny fall.
Feelings in this life is a crime unforgivable.

You cannot kill the devil in man or revive the angel.
Tomorrow the nights will fold you in the darkness of perdition.
Tomorrow the dust will capture you, there will be no feelings.

How heavy and cruel was the burden of my dreams and pains.
So, take us to perdition, perhaps we forget and be forgotten.
Let the holy curtain for, we had enough care and despair.

(*Complete Works*, vol. 1, 1971, pp. 568–570; orig. pub. July 19, 1946)

7. CITY OF LOVE

In the depth of life's desert, there, over the blaze of sand,
Where the winds boom, there is a town among the hills.

In its midst there is a river, surrounded by rocks and wilds,
And banks with no shade, no woods, no perfumes.

The water looks calm, but beyond it is deep pain.
Its waves are lethal poison, though they look sweetly right.

Many a barque was misled by its fairies and sights.
Many a dream was destroyed by its waves and poisons.

The other bank suggests beauty and enchantment,
But when you approach it, you find the storm of death.

Nothing is seen on its rocks except thorns and remains.
No sound is heard except the din of its worms and eagles.

Night there is fears and incessant scruples.
Forever convulsed by ambiguous cries and sighs.

O frightened knocker on the door, return and do not stay here.
This beauty will turn into blood and stagnant water.

All these banks have is distress and grief.
So be aware! Poisons and daggers are prepared.

Your eyes' light do not cast on their darkness.
Your youth hopes do not bury in their life's distress.

Your beating heart protect against their sinful dust.
What have you gained from life, to seek protection in its darkness?

Return, go back to the desert flames, escape the city heat.
Do not cast your heart in fire, but listen to a sad poetess.

(*Complete Works*, vol. 1, 1971, pp. 568–570; orig. pub. July 19, 1946)

8. INSPIRATION ISLAND

Take me to the distant world,
O Boat of magic and eternity.

And go with my heart shores
That inspire the heart with poems.

The Inspiration Island from afar,
Looks like a distant hope.

The sound on its shore is wet,
Sipping from the cool Tigris.

The sweet morning in its sky,
Is there hope for a lonesome poet?

So go, my boat, with my soul.
It is time my lute should wake up.

It is time for poetry to sing
With the laughing, flittering dream.

My dream, which I turned into a song,
My existence rejoices at its magic.

My poetess, look closely,
This is the island of poetry and song.

Its two banks gleamed from afar,
A hope of the new world.

If the two eyes winked away from it,
The hopes would call them to return.

So smile, daughter of songs,
To the extending, charming shore.

And halt the tired boat,
Under the rays of the scattered light.

The lute, poetry, and songs,
My poetess, sing and sing some more.

Lifetime has laughed, and calmed down
Are the storms of despair and misery.

Despair turned into good news,
And hopes. What a feast!

(*Complete Works*, vol. 1, 1971, pp. 5–9; orig. pub. 1944)

9. MEMORY TREE

I passed by it in the dark evening,
And settled under its shade.
I gazed at its green leaves,
When my dejected soul was dark.
It raised in my heart the night of memories,
And I filled my tune with its woe.
I made its trunk my backrest
And all around it turned my sorrows.

I remembered, as my heart was in grief,
My standing in its enchanting shade.
As if the long nights have not passed,
Over my distant bygone past.
I stood to wipe off my hot tears,
And cry of my relentless pain.
Relating to its shade my tale
And that of my disloyal poet

I told it that depressing tale,
As in my hand I held a blade.
Passing with it in my sorrow,
Over its faithful peaceful trunk,
Oh, for my hand that injured its trunk,
And sheered its bright flowers off,
As if, by that, I wounded life,
And punished its cheating destinies.

The lengthy years then passed by me,
And I beheld my usual day,
In which I saw my distant grief,
Felt by my sad and passionate heart.
I said to my heart, let us go and turn
Around it to raise your dormant grief,
To ask it today about its wound,
Has it not been healed by time?

I came back to it, as if the years
Have not passed by me with their pain.
My heart has been imprisoned still,
My soul's fire has been burning
Again, its shade can shadow me,
Its flowers on my heart are tender.
How normal it was, as it pardoned
My hand, though its vengeance it still holds.

I turned to ask about its wound:
has it been healed by destiny?
I saw nothing but life so green,
But no sign was in it of any wound.
But for the wounds of my sad heart,
They still complain of absence long.
I wonder at injuring time,
When will it apologize?

(*Complete Works*, vol. 1, 1971, pp. 14–16; orig. pub. 1944)

10. A YEAR LATER

A year has passed, my poet,
     Since I saw you on that gloomy morning.
A year has passed, and my thirsty eye
     Was not graced then by seeing you, so my gloom would abate.
Nights pass, followed by days,
     In their monotonous, boring slow pace.
And I am all yearning, my longing increases,
     And my soul is in a stormy flame.
A thirst for life fills my senses,
     And fire is my shed tears.
With sparks of melancholy that, on my forehead,
     Painted a veil of pallor.

A year has passed, who said so?
     Am I in a dream built by my stricken fancy?
Is it an illusion, which I thought a whole year,
     Whose lights the vile time extinguished?
A year it has passed, and I did not meet you, what?
     How did carers keep me alive?
How could I stay alive, when you were absent,
     But gloom did not kill me?
The grievous inhaling, in the still of the night,
     Did not the breeze convey to you?
The distraction, which killed my feelings,
     Have not the stars told you about?

I still remember the morning,
     Which passed as dew over my broken heart.
A year ago, in the boisterous long street,
     As the sun was of ether purity,
The sweet chance brought us together, there,
     As destiny was inadvertently absent,
And we met, we did not smile, I did not tell you
     Of what lies in my pressed heart.

A moment, then cruel time put an end
    To my enchanted dream.
I went right, you went left, and nothing remained
    Except my outbreak and fiery feelings.

The entire year passed, and every day
    I received the morning with dreams.
Every day, I say: O, my heart, thirsty
    For clear skies, do not be impatient with clouds.
Perhaps the blind chances will have mercy on us,
    This morning, after darkness.
It will not hurt destinies, in the night,
    To receive you once with a smile.
So life will, again, run in you,
    And the hushed tunes we wake up.
Feelings will run mad, in your very depth,
    Alive and free from pains.

A year has passed and the silly clock
Rang ten, and my sorrows woke up.
Tuesday did not restore you, to the desires
Of my torn, pining soul.
A year has passed, like a dream that passed,
Over the eyelids of wakeful poet.
A year has passed, leaving nothing but
A sad tune, of very deep tone.
Nothing but a bitter, thirsty smile,
And the beats of my bewildered heart,
Nothing but a shade of silence and pining,
Sitting on my thirsty eyelids.   (June 6, 1945)

(*Complete Works*, vol. 1, 1971, pp. 620–625)

11. RAINY NIGHT

Now, my star, you disappear, though it is not yet the setting-time?
Now, while the fair night casts your light on the fields,
And the flowers and the night are elated with your fair rise?
As the river and banks laugh under the palm trees.

Now you decided to go! What tragedy for the withering beauty!
Oh, my star held by the hand of comprehensive fog.
Oh, night philosopher, oh secret of distrait existence,
In vain are songs to the lights of a setting star.

In vain I stayed up the night, gazing, overwhelmed by anguish,
Taking the last look at your languid light,
Composing elegies on your departing youth,
Weaving the light of my tears, for every setting star.

For pity, my pretty star, when is my night end?
When will the clouds be clear, and my gloom end?
My heart desires to feel silence under my canopy of trees.
As my eyes traverse the space with guitar in my hand.

I have been waiting for calm, but there is only the rain's echo,
And the wind, moaning to the evening, among the trees.
No bird is fluttering in the fields, no fragrance, no flowers,
Nothing but thunder, telling of the human grief.

Out of the dark rose moans of the branches' dove,
Whose nest was blown away by the wind, spoiling her dear abode.
Perplexed, with shivering wings, wounded under the dark,
Pity, Lord of storms, enough is the pouring rain for us.

Where is the fair space, the clarity, the star-light?
Who gathered the grim rain, and sent the clouds, in the grim night?
Oh, wind, be kind to me, to the bowers and vines,
Be kind to the meadow dove, so wearied by cares.

In my heart were hopes that you betrayed, O winds,
There were charms in this evening that you effaced,
There were vine canopies in the fair meadow that you withered,
There were stars in the sky seas that you turned off.

In the grim night I remained, listening to the grim rain,
On my mouth was the strange tune, shaped by my strange heart,
Through the windows peeps to me the horrible night darkness.
In the high feed my fireplace, as the flames will die now.
The storm has destroyed my two windows, and the light was gone,
And now there is no light around me except the lightning,
O horizon uproar, oh, sky rain,
Now I plead for sleep until tomorrow, so farewell!

(*Complete Works*, vol. 1, 1971, pp. 634–637; November 6, 1946)

From *Sparks and Ashes*
(1949)

12. LOST UTOPIA

A lost echo, like a remote mirage
Attracts my soul, day and night.
I sleep on its eternal sound,
It wakes me by its pleasant song,
An echo never like any other,
Sung by a secret guitar.
If heard by my life, it would fall
In yearning, and call it a thousand times.
At its repeat dies every wound
In my heart, and every hope would shine.
My feeling would move in ecstasy,
Numbed by the dream of Utopia.
A dream in my blood is Utopia,
I die and live by its name,
I fancied it a land of fragrance,
On a horizon's secret I could not guess.
There, across a distant void,
The planets melt in its magic.
The light dies, but its color
And fragrance cannot be grasped.
There, where all bonds disappear,
And thought is freed from its bondage.
Where the eyes of life do sleep,
There is where spreads Utopia.

Utopia is where the light stays
And does not set or wane the sun,
Where violet aroma stays alive.
And where narcissus does not wither,
Where life can flow with wholesome nectar
And cups are never empty.
Where limits of time are lost
Where stars can never drowse.

There, life is an extent of youth,
With its elation souls are full,
And there, the spring remains a spring,
Shading the men of Utopia.

There, where Scheherazade came up
With tales she sang a thousand nights.
And where Diana drives the light
And Narcissus his shadow worships,
There, Utopia is a twilight fog,
The like of which was never seen.
Surrounded by eternal fragrance,
Offering her the tunes and kisses.
She lives indefinitely drunk,
By the echo of waning songs.
On the shore so full of star-light,
Which I call Utopia shore.

One evening there I toured around,
Accompanied by a mirage-like form:
I felt its steps upon the sand,
But saw nothing except some clouds.
And in my body moved a life,
Flying, with my soul, above the land.
Before me was a strange passage
Covered by puffs of fog.
On both sides spread a gulf
With some islands and heights.
Dreaming, I shouted: Where am I?
The Echo said: By Utopia.

Deep in my soul I felt madness,
A yearning like a sea so deep,
Wishing the strange way could lead me,
To the deep and desired land.
To that eternal horizon,

Where lives the gentle Apollo.
I walk and walk, and nothing look
Before me but extending roads
Thirsty for existence rare,
On which melt dew and lightning.
A startling thirst, and finally,
I woke up to see no Utopia.

In another dream, I was traveling,
On a shore of pebbles and sands,
Strange, strange, like the color of ether
Surrounded by a fancy horizon.
It led my tired feet ahead,
To a rock eternally fixed.
Climbing it is a waning hope,
As even shadows there could slip.
I stood down by its feet, and moaned,
On a wretched, untenable hope.
I wondered what could be behind it.
The sound replied: Utopia.

In a third dream, I thought myself
At its large marble gate,
Staring with unconfined elation,
I could go mad, or I could fly.
Do I really see the gate?
Its boards were draped with silk,
I stepped in reverence and in awe,
My eyes had a glimpse of peaceful dreams,
Elated, I knocked on the door,
Not answer but bitter silence.
I shouted with a restrained voice:
Let me die at the gates of Utopia.

My life went by; it went in vain,
And nothing can the yearning quench.

In vain I crossed the life deserts,
In vain I dragged the years' fetters.
I still am crossing the silent wastes,
Asking all men about their secret.
Waiting is heavy on my heart.
So I sink in deep despair.
I tried the solace in something:
A wood, a valley, or shady trees.
Minutes and I despair and shout:
There is nothing like Utopia.

I remain attracted by my hopes,
To the remote, eternal horizon.
I dream, I dream, but do not wake
Except to dream another dream.
I kiss its walls in my fancy,
And ask the wider space about it,
And ask the pouring fragrance, too,
I ask you, dew, and mountain ice,
I ask till my question dies
Upon my lips, and the song withers.
And when I die, my heart will have
Made an appointment with Utopia.

(*Complete Works*, vol. 2, 1971, pp. 35–44; orig. pub. 1948)

13. WHEN THE PAST REVIVED

Yesterday, at night, the secret images were various,
Alluding my drowsy presence, yesterday was dead.
I thought I shrouded it, one evening,
And I took support from my pride.
In the sleep darkness, my soul heard a sound,
It was not a dream of mythical covers,
Created by a desire, behind my feelings.
It was something, it was in the lull of night, your own voice.

That voice that my hearing knows well,
The voice of a past, which died and left nothing,
Except fragments of a pale disgust,
Which settled in the bottom of my silent heart,
Except memory fragments, of a love that was alive.
Years ago, it has passed away and gone.
Years ago, and now it has become a memory,
Folded by the past and buried forever.

That voice, which passed by my hearing yesterday
Was one day a desire sobbing in my soul.
It was a dream melted in my tears,
It was a love misled by my hopes.
Then, on its memory, I smashed my guitar and cup,
When I lost them in the fog,
And stumbled with the remains of my youth,
And crumbled, on my hopes and pleasure.

Two lengthy months passed languidly,
My lifetime was a ruin colored by sunset,
Phantoms pass the night in silence,
And the owl lives in their misery shade.
Whenever confusion tours with me, in this strange underground,
Memory throws out its hands to me.
Its color creates a world of my terror
And moves the dead chord in my dismayed heart.

Two cursed years of my love years passed by,
Their claws tore my soul and heart.
They did not leave even a sail of hope,
They left nothing but my dignity,
And fragments of memories of a wolf cruelty.
In them is my soul's, all my yesterday's color,
My yesterday, which settled in my deep senses.
It sensed in them the echo of the sound that whispered near me.

It is the past, then, that came to live anew,
It came, then, knocking at the doors of my distraction.
Sorry, my phantom, return to your dust,
You can no longer knock at my door.
No longer join us except the limits.
A pit, deeper than your sin!
What is left of you with me, except this?
Except a memory that, one day, crossed my life?

(*Complete Works*, vol. 2, 1971, pp. 54–57)

14. THE SERPENT

Which way should I go? I am bored with the roads,
Weary with the meadows,
And the secret insistent enemy
Is still following my steps, so where is the escape?
Passages and roads, going with songs
To every strange horizon,
The roads of life,
The tunnels in the dark nights,
The corners of the arid day,
I have all toured, and my obstinate secret enemy
Is steady, like ice-mountains
Of the remote north.
Firm, like firming stars,
In the eyes deprived of sleep,
And attacked by worries,
With wounds of insomnia,
Steadfast, like steadfast time,
At the hour of waiting,
Whenever my steps flee more,
It oversteps the peaks
And brings me what the day's efforts
Have destroyed of my memory bonds.
I will not seek release
From my bonds, and what release
When my fearful enemy
Has two eyes that spit autumn
On a spirit that seeks a spring!
And beyond that translucent fog
There is that horrible serpent,
That monster! What release
Can it get from its hands-shadow
On my cold forehead?
How can I escape,
When its spiteful eye unbearable future lashes

Pour on my way a dead, unbearable future?
Which way should I go? Which tern
Should close the door against my doubtful enemy?
It challenges hope,
And scornfully guffaws at my horrible gloom.
It does not feel weeping.
Where? Where should I hide?
My constant, monotonous escape
No longer responds
To my call of horror.
What use is calling?
Is there a nearby refuge place?
Or a distant one. . . . I shall go,
Even if it were beyond the sky,
Or behind the limits of hope.
Then, one evening, I hear the voice:
"Go on, this is a deep road
Overstepping the limits of space,
Where you should not hear the serpent's humming.
It is an abysmal labyrinth,
Perhaps built by a hand in ancient times,
For a curious prince.
Then the Prince died, and the road remained
For the hands of loss."
I hear the voice all over the place,
So I walk, perhaps I wake
From the nights of my saucy, eternal nightmare.
Perhaps my enemy will miss the way.
How nice it is to walk with no dead steps behind me.
Stretching with its pallid echoes,
In the bends of the long way.
It will not come,
Will not come, even if it crossed the impossible.
It will never come;
My innocent heart will not see it
Once more, raising the winds

To block my way.
In the quiet of the morning
It will never come,
It will never come!
Then I hear a spiteful guffaw:
It came. What a loss was my broken hope
In the night of the blind labyrinth
Then I feel the giant hand
Pressing cold and horror on my naive calm
With its frozen fingers.
It has come. . . . What use is going?
I should say farewell to my short dream,
And return with its cold corpse.

Then life goes on and on,
And my secret stubborn enemy
Is behind every new road,
In the pallid dejection nights,
Behind every dawn,
I see it peeping at me with the expected,
With my distant past
In the wider space.
Which way is to escape
From my obstinate enemy?
It is like destiny,
Everlasting, it is eternal.
Everlasting.

(*Complete Works*, vol. 2, 1971, pp. 57–81; orig. pub. 1948)

15. MYTHS

"For my friend Daisy Al-Ameer, in honor of one evening when
we philosophized everything, including chairs, tables, and curtains."

They said: Life.
It is the color of a dead person's eyes.
It is the footsteps of a watchful murderer.
Its wrinkled days
Are like a poisoned coat, dripping death.
Its dreams are the smiles of an ogress of drugged eyes.
Beyond its smile is death.

They said: Hope.
It is the site of the thirsty, when he sees the cups,
In a picture on the wall.
It is that frowning color
On the face of a sparrow whose nest was spoiled.
So it wept and flew away,
And stayed waiting for the morning,
Hoping a miracle will restore
The ruins of its ruined nest anew.

They said: Bliss.
I looked for it in the sunken eyes,
In the misery story written on some faces,
In Time consumed by its years,
In flowers' fragrance threatened by fading,
In a pretty star endangered by setting.
They said: The bliss, but I could not find it.
Has it folded its future and died?

They said: Quietude.
A foolish myth, brought in by the inanimate,
Or listens with the ears and leaves the soul under the ashes,
Who did not hear the cries sent by the fence,

And by the paper fragments torn in the ruins,
By the dust and the old room seats,
By the glass, covered with cobweb,
And a coat on the wall.

They said: Youth.
When I asked about it, they told me about years,
Coming to dissipate the fog.
They talked about a paradise beyond the mirage,
They talked about an oasis for the tired,
I reached it to find tomorrow's dreams
Crucified by the closed lock.

They said: Immortality.
I found it a shadow, stretching languidly
Over the graves where life shrinks.
I found it an utterance on some lips
That they sang while wailing over their past
And lowering it into the graves,
Singing it while dying. . . . What disdain!

They said: The Hearts.
I found doors leading in suffocation
To graveyards where feeling was buried
And where the future of fancy died.
Their sticky walls devour beauty
And spit unbearable ugliness.
I escaped, pallid. Are these hearts, then?
What hopes failure! I will not return.

They said: The Eyes.
I found eyelids without vision
And found eyelashes tied to stones
And caves draped with curtains of suspicion,
Blind, except to evils, though called eyes.
I knew thousands with eyes of glass sheets:

Blue, like the sky, with darkness behind the blue.
They said, and they said. . . .
Their words' repetition was chewed by the wind.
In a world of empty sounds monitored by extinction.
The tired without rest,
The lost without end.
They said, I said, and there is nothing left to say.
What myth! What irony of fancy!

(*Complete Works*, vol. 2, 1971, pp. 82–87; orig. pub. 1948)

16. IN THE NORTHERN MOUNTAINS

Return with us, O train,
Darkness is horrible here, stillness is heavy.
Return with us, the distance is huge,
The road is long.
The nights are short.
Return with us, the winds are wailing beyond the shadows,
The wolves' howling behind the mountain
Sounds like a grievous call in human hearts.
Return with us, as on the slope
There is a sad, gloomy phantom
Whose footprints there on every dawn are seen.
Every dawn that passed here, with gloom and yearning,
Is the phantom of mortal exile.
In the said northern mountains,
The phantom of mortal loneliness.
Return with us, we are bored with roaming
In the mountain slopes, and turned frightened
That the absence nights may be long
And the wolves' howling may cover our voice,
And to return may be difficult for us.
Return with us to the south.
There, behind the mountains there are hearts,
Return with us to those we left in the fog.
Every hand is waving in yearning and gloom,
Every hand is a heart.
Return with us, O train!
We are bored with roaming.
Separation became long.
There is a whisper, over there,
Lisping behind every road,
In the huge mountain passes,
And behind the clouds,
In the quiver of the pine trees, in the pallid village,
In the howling of the jackals, in the setting stars,

In the pastures, over there, there is a roaming voice,
Whispering to return.
For there are other homes there,
Other pastures,
Other hearts.
There, there are eyes that refuse to sleep,
Hands that hold the burning night,
Lips that repeat our names in the dark,
Hearts that listen to our footsteps in gloom,
Calling to the stars in silence and gloom:
"When will the fugitives remember us, O stars?
And when will they return?"

One moment, we shall return!
Night will not see us here. We shall return.
We shall fold the mountains,
The heaps of hills,
The northern nights will not see us
Here, once more
We shall return,
Wide space will not feel
The fire of our sighs, in the horrible evening,
In the still, horrible evening.

Return with us, O northern train,
For there, beyond the mountains,
There are the fair faces, covered by the nights.
Return with us,
Return to the loving arms,
In the palm tree shades,
Where our past days
Have been waiting for long,
Stood in waiting,
Expecting the return of the train,
To walk with the others,
Where our days ask the passers-by,

One by one in yearning:
"When is the fugitives' return?"

Let us return, an old song
Around us is whispering of return.
How lovely is return,
After this painful wandering,
In the arid mountain passes
Where the wolves howl
Let us return; the night is ice cold.
And there, beyond the spacious void,
There are warm arms.
Let us return, as the mountains
Are baring their dark night.
And there, beyond the obscure dark,
Is the voice of our beloved, in the deep dark,
Pulsing with deep yearning.
Their voice is laden with gentle reproach.
Their voice was echoed by the mountain passes.
Their voice, in the stillness of the place,
Circulates like Time.
Let us return, before the serpent
Decides on a long, long departure
From the palm-tree shades,
From our dear ones beyond the silent waste.
Return with us, O train!
The nights are short
And there, our beloved ones are languidly waiting.   (Sarsang, 1948)

(*Complete Works*, vol. 2, 1971, pp. 124–130)

17. UTOPIA IN THE MOUNTAINS

"Presented to my sister Iḥsān, who witnessed with me its birth near
the icy water spring, running down the colorful Sarsang rocks."

Burst, O springs,
With water, and melted rays.
Burst with light, with colors, over the pallid village,
In that valley, draped with night and stillness.
Burst in tunes
Over the spreading slopes among the hills,
In the bend, where shades wave,
Under the spreading branches.
Burst in beauty,
And raise Utopia in the mountains,
Utopia of the mountain-tops' trees,
Of the water's murmur,
Utopia of tunes,
Pulsing with life.
Burst, run on the rocky slopes,
Where the butterflies float,
In ecstasy, shivering.
Burst where the birds sleep,
In a paradise of perfumes,
Where the mountain foot is covered by a dense forest
Of piny rustling.
Burst pure over the slope pebbles,
By the bend of the fearful, deep valley,
In the shades of the leafy soft walnut,
Under the spread of trees.
Burst in the morning.
Burst, scraping like winds.
Burst at sunset,
And raise Utopia of hearts,
Of every heart not pressed by grudge,
Not defiled by stagnation,

Of every deep poetic heart,
Not wallowed in life sins,
Of every gentle heart,
Deep in its dreams, not waking
Except to a remote dream,
That has no limits.
A dream challenging the future
Of every heart that cannot stand stagnation,
Or the screeching of fetters.

Burst, white over the rocks,
In color and light, challenging all human filth.
Burst, the slope will not be bored.
Flow over the sleepy,
And drown the drowsy unjust.
Flood over the dead,
Over the hearts that shield no yearning,
Over eyes and purified by weeping,
Over souls that do not feel the sky,
Over hands that have no dignity.
Run far away in the hungry villages
Of the naked and the barefooted,
Where life, hearing, cannot catch
Anything but the cries of imploring souls
And the howling of wolves
At the bend of said wretched valley.
At the lofty plateau,
Where the eye of years cannot see
But the grief of the tired
Caravans driven by the wretched
In a paradise of bliss.
Caravans of the hungry
In the valley of fertile soil,
Caravans of the thirsty
Groping for the mirage,
As water overwhelmed the slipping years.

Caravans of boredom
Denied the mountain purity, by toil.
Caravans that spit out the axes peel
Others for cups,
For sleep and dreams under the shade,
Half-dead, that do not feel beauty.

Burst, O waters.
Burst over people's graves,
Burst in the rocks,
And record the tragedy of this life
On the forehead of destiny.
The village has always been
A tale mixed with pain,
The wind related its misery
To the pale morning.
Burst, flow, and cover the tops,
And cover the story with nullity.
Do not remember this sad song.
It was nothing but an echo of a whisper,
Listened to by the years
For a moment, and then it sank in silence.   (Sarsang, 1948)

(*Complete Works*, vol. 1, 1971, pp. 152–158)

18. THE THREAD TIED TO THE CYPRESS TREE

(1)

In the dark, street blackness, and deaf silence,
Where there is no color except that of darkening nights,
Where the oleander tree loosens its gloom,
A shadow on the surface of the earth,
A voice told me a story, then it receded,
And faded in the night its lips.

(2)

A story of the love, which your heart thought dead,
But it is still an explosion and life.
Tomorrow, desire will press you to me,
You will call me to exhaustion,
Memory will press on your chest,
A burden of madness, so you can touch nothing,
Anything, a dream, a gentle word,
Anything, the road will call you,
And you wake up.
The night will see you alone, on the road,
Asking the distant past
To return.
The dreaming street and the oleander
Will see you walking,
Your eyes colored by excitement and delight,
With love and feelings on your face,
Everything in your very depth is painted there.
And I, myself, can see,
From my dark, distant, drowsy place,
Can see the happy dream
Behind your eyes, defeatedly calling
And finally, you see the house,
Our house, where we met,
When our love was that naive child,
Its color in our lips,
Its youth quivers in our hands.

(3)

You see the house and remain still for a moment:
"Here is the house, as it used to be, there,
Still covered by oleander,
Shaded by bitter orange and luxuriant cypress.
And here is our seat. . . . What do I feel?
Confusion in my very depth, whisper,
Warning, challenging my heart dream.
Perhaps she was. . . . But why is my horror?
She is keeping our love promise.
She is still yearning,
And will meet me with her greetings as before,
And she would meet me. . . ."
And you walk confidently and calmly,
In the quiet and dark corridor, you walk,
Sneering at the warning of illusion.
"Here, I have returned, having dropped the heaps of my sins.
Here, I can see your eyes peeping.
Perhaps you were behind the door, covered by shade.
Here I have returned, here is the staircase.
Here is the door of the dark color, why do I recoil?
A minute, then I see her.
A minute, then I feel her footsteps.
Well, let me knock on the door. . . . Moments pass on,
And the door squeaks with melancholy tones.
You see in the dark corridor a pale face,
Frozen, reflecting a setting shadow.
"Has she. . . ?" And your husky voice fades in a sad tone.
"Do not say she. . . ."
                    "What madness!
You dreamer, whom are you asking about?
She died."
              Two moments passed.
And you still look as if you have not heard the exciting voice.
Frozen, staring all around,
Distrait, your eyes fixed to a short thread,

Tied to the cypress tree, you do not know when?
And why? It was not there
Two months ago. Your lips were about
To ask the sister about that short thread.
Why did they tie it? And when?
The sound rings in your ear: "She died. . . ."
And you stare vacantly,
To see the thread as ropes of ice,
Tied by arms that vanished, and were overwhelmed by death,
Thousands of centuries ago.
And you see the sad face, magnified in your eyes
By clouds of horror. "She died."

(4)

"She died." . . . An utterance without meaning,
An echo of an empty hammer that rises, then vanishes.
You are not concerned with its monotonous repetition.
All that you see now is the strange thread.
Did she tie it? Then rises that boring sound
 Of "She died" thundering, not vanishing,
Filling the night with cries and thunder.
"She died," an echo, clearly whispered by the sound,
A call reverberated by the darkness,
Related by the cypress trees, in a deep voice.
"She died" is what the storms say.
"She died" is an echo, crying in the deep stars.
And you can almost hear it now, behind the veins.

(5)

The sound of "She died" was ringing everywhere.
This empty hammer in the ear of Time.
The sound "she died" is suffocating like a serpent.
Every letter is a nerve, panting in your chest in horror.
A vision of a red gallows without a heart.
An attack of a twitching paw, snapping fiercely.
An echo of a hellish, harsh voice,

Is this empty hammer: She died,
She died, and the world does not hold her any more.
In vain you ask darkness about her.
In vain you listen to her footsteps.
In vain you look for her in the moon.
In vain you dream that one day you will see her
Anywhere except in the depth of memory.
She disappeared behind the stars.
And turned a blink of a dream.

(6)

Then, here you are, without movements,
Tired, about to collapse on the passage floor.
Your deranged eyes, tied over there,
To a thread tied to the cypress, folding a thousand secrets.
That strange thread,
That dubious riddle,
It is all that is left of your withered, melancholy love.

(7)

The night sees you walking to return:
The thread in your hand, the shiver, and the thundering nerve.
"She died," and you go distrait,
Fondling with the thread, folding, and turning
Its end on your thumb, as there is nothing else left.
All that deep love has left you
Is this thread and the utterance of "She died."
And every other whisper was folded out.

(*Complete Works*, vol. 2, 1971, pp. 185–194; orig. pub. 1948)

19. THE CHOLERA

The night calmed down.
Listen to the beat of the sighs' echo
In the depth of darkness, under silence, on the dead.
Cries are rising, confused.
Grief is blowing, inflamed,
Stumbles in it the groans' echo.
Boiling is in every heart,
Sorrows are in the quiet hut,
A soul in every darkness cries,
A voice in every place weeps.
This is what death has lacerated,
Death, death, death,
Oh! for the Nile grief of what death has done.

The dawn is up,
Listen to the beat of the walkers' footsteps
In the silence of the dawn, hearken, look at the mourners' procession.
Ten dead, twenty.
Do not count, listen to the mourners,
Listen to the voice of the poor child.
Dead, dead, the count is lost,
Dead, dead; no tomorrow is left.
In every spot there is a body mourned by a grieved.
No moment of calm, no silence.
This is what the hand of death has done:
Death, death, death.
Humanity complains, complains of what death has committed.

The cholera
In the cave of horror with remains,
In the cruel perpetual silence, where death is a cure,
The cholera woke up,
In rancor bursting, enraged.
It went down the bright, cheerful valley,

Shrieking, perturbed, and mad,
Not hearing the voice of the mourners.
In every place its paw left its echoes.
In the farmer's hut, in the house,
There is nothing but the shrieks of death.
Death, death, death.
In the cruel figure of cholera death takes revenge.
Silence is bitter,
There is nothing but the echo of supplications,
Even the gravedigger dropped down, and no help is left.
The mosque prayer-caller is dead.
Who will, then, inter the dead?
Nothing is left but moaning and sighs.
The child has no father or mother,
Crying out of a burning heart.
Tomorrow it will certainly be snatched by the vicious ailment.
Oh! cholera phantom, you have left
Nothing but the griefs of death.
Death, death, death.
Oh, Egypt, my feeling was lacerated by what death has done.

(*Complete Works*, vol. 2, 1971, pp. 136–140; orig. pub. 1947)

From *The Wave's Nadir*
(1957)

20. TO THE NEW YEAR

O year! Do not come near our homes;
We are here but visions,
Of the phantom world,
Disavowed by humans.
The night and the past escape us,
Destiny is not aware of us,
We lead the life of wandering phantoms,
We are the ones who walk with no remembrance,
No dream, no shining desires, no hopes.
Our eyes' horizons are ashes,
Those stagnant lakes in the silent faces.
We have the speechless foreheads,
Without bolts or flash.
We are the ones bared of feelings, our lips are pale,
We are the escapees from Time to Nullity,
Ignorant of repentance grief.
We live in the luxury of palaces
But stay in need of feelings
And memories.
We live, but life is unaware of us.
We live, but do not complain,
And we are ignorant of weeping,
Of death, of birth, of the meaning of the sky.

* * *

O year! Proceed, here is the road
Leading your steps.
In vain we hope you could wake up.
We, who have veins of reeds,
White or green. We are devoid of feelings,
Grief we do not know, and anger,
And what they mean by saying
That conscience may flare.
We wish we could die to be rejected by the graves.

We wish if Time
Could find its way to us, like the others.
If we could date by years,
If we could be tied to place,
If the doors of lofty palaces
Could bring our hearts anything, other than air,
If we could proceed with life,
Walking, feeling, seeing, sleeping,
Reached by winter snow,
And our forehead wrapped by darkness.
Ah! If we could feel as the others feel,
If melodies could beat us at times,
And pain attack.
If memory, or hope, or remorse
Would one day block our indolence.
If we could fear madness,
Or stillness could raise our gloom.
If our rest could be disturbed by departure,
Or shock, or a grief of impossible love.
Oh! If we could die as the others die.   (January 1, 1950)

(*Complete Works*, vol. 2, 1971, pp. 251–254)

21. THE FUGITIVES

Till when shall we go on wandering in distant lands?
Mirage trifles with us,
One low land turns us to another,
And the road bend deceives us.

* * *

Why did we come? The sea asks us: What do we want?
The wind carriages follow us, and repeat,
Repeating the question.
But there is no answer except the boredom lines
On our silent faces in the long nights.
We flee, but they catch us anew.

* * *

The horizon asks us: Where do we travel? Where do we go?
From what did we escape? And why? To what end?
In our silence
There are hearts beating; the fall of hopes
On our distress is unbearable joy.
So let us look for a wound of a small grief.

* * *

As we walk, we hear the night deriding our secret,
Following us in the dark, instigating the winds against us.
The road asks:
Why do we wander in this deep, deep world,
Followed by our past, our visions, and a friend's face?
Until when shall we flee from our shadow?

* * *

In our walk in darkness, we see the moon's derision.
The cool light angers us, and some trees
Block our way.
The sunset ridicules us,

Saying we are searching for the impossible
And that, despite our hopes, we are human.

* * *

From the sides of the paths, we hear one evening
An echo whispering in the night that we are. . . . Cowards.
We fear the sunset.
We depart, not out of desire for departure
But to flee from ourselves, from a long struggle,
From the fact that we are still outsiders.

* * *

And here we are, where we started,
Wandering in the terrible dark;
A winter dying, questions not answered by a spring.
Bewildered eyes.
Our future asks us who we are,
And leaves us, in the fog of centuries, our past.
O night, O sea, where are we lost?   (USA, January 1951)

(*Complete Works*, vol. 2, 1971, pp. 302–305)

22. WHAT DOES THE RIVER SAY?

"To the friend who asked me one evening:
'What does the river say?'"

What does the river say?
　　　　　A tale.
It weaves it of moonlight dance.
It weaves it of gentle courting,
With which the palm trees humor the slope,
Of a lamplight that feeds the night
With warmth and excites the trees
Of the fall of light moving beat,
Opening the river chest at night.

* * *

What does the river say?
　　　　　A song,
Old, a daughter of long nights.
Once a lover sang its sorrow,
And the night was drunk, on a cup of beauty,
Laden with warmth, retaining still
In its tunes some of the camels' yearning,
The camelback submission, under the night,
The heavy footstep fall of the cameleers.

* * *

What does the river say?
　　　　　An anthem
From Babylon, elate with incense-odor,
The monks' procession, in a temple
That the Tigris and rocks hide its secret.
Memoirs of the night and the sun,
(The sun city) behind the ages,
Of Hammurabi and his love,
And what was covered by the treacherous book of Time.

* * *

What does the river say?
                          Do not ask.
Let the secret cover thick and deep.
If the Tulip uncovered its riddles,
There would be no sense of its gentle fragrance.   (July 27, 1950)

(*Complete Works*, vol. 2, 1971, pp. 306–309)

23. THE OTHER PERSON

Should you come tomorrow, crossing yesterday's limits, to my promised
  tomorrow,
And happily sing your arrival, even the crossway and the closed door,
And I met you, searching in you for the remains of my lost yesterday,
    Should you come and I could not find you in my tunes,
    And from you peeped on my soul the other person.

* * *

The other person, from the depths of buried months of loss,
Woven by the minutes of those arrogant, criminal days,
And settled in his eyes their slow passage and frightened visions,
    I shall look in you for the past, confidently,
    My heating longing is surprised by the other person.

* * *

And there, on the sensitive face, of lively silence, I see two shadows,
Instead of one, in your sensitive eyes, I feel two.
The two persons meet me together, and in vain I hope to separate the
  two opposites.
    And I shall ask what the two years have left me
    Of your face, and the answer is the forehead, of the other person.

* * *

This foolish second person shall dwell even in the smiles.
He would instill his cold in the gentleness of your voice, in the soft tones.
He will glance at me viciously, hidden, even behind words.
    To whom shall I complain, about this devilish creature,
    When the first in you was effaced by the hand of the second person.

(*Complete Works*, vol. 2, 1971, pp. 336–338; orig. pub. October 9, 1951)

24. DISAPPOINTMENT

We returned to the land, and the road
        Was our former road.
Fatigue did not leave us a glare
From the fresh leafy yesterday,
        Flaring across the visions.

* * *

We returned to find the uplands and fields
        As we left them.
The sun was still nourishing the plains,
Followed by the slow and lazy night,
        Effacing its remains.

* * *

People here are still planting
        And reaping cares.
The sun knows that they are still dipping
Their sins in the darkness of centuries
        And glimpse at the stars.

* * *

And we are still as we used to be,
        The same old fools.
The night goes by, sneering at us,
The dawn relates to the night,
        That we drink what we are served.

* * *

And yesterday, with the departing caravan,
        We proceeded with the others,
Crossing thousands of arid highlands.
When the caravan brought us to a halt,
        After the years have passed.

* * *

Our disappointment went mad,
    And what was hoped was gone.
Our distress and desire exhausted us,
As beyond the highlands and love,
    Lies our former spot.

(*Complete Works*, vol. 2, 1971, pp. 361–364; orig. pub. May 1, 1952)

25. PHANTOMS' PRAYER

The cold clock on the tower fidgeted
In the hush of darkness,
And stuck out a hand of brass,
A hand like a myth, carefully moved by Buddha,
The hand of the upright man,
On the tower clock in his eternal silence,
Staring like a melancholy face.
His eyes shoot a torrent of thick darkness
On the dormant castle,
On the dead whose eyes do not die
But stay staring, with uttering silence.
The hand of the upright man said:
"Prayer, prayer."

* * *

A life moved,
In the tired guards, there, on the tower,
So, they slowly dragged on the land
Their tired shadows, bent by years,
Their shadows in the deep sad darkness,
And the hand of the upright man
Turned to point: "Prayer, prayer."
The sound is lost in the growing din,
The echo of the approaching guard procession
Knocks on every door and screams at the sleepers,
And emerges a phantom at every door,
A thin, pale phantom,
Dragging the ashes of years,
Night can almost weep
On his sad skull face.

* * *

Their procession moved in silence,
Treading on the strange roads, not realizing
Why they are proceeding, what would happen?

Around them twisted the dark roads,
Creeping serpents and fangs.
They moved pallidly, dragging their secrets.
Their voices whisper a horrible chant,
The chant of those whose eyes do not die,
A chant for that wondrous god,
And a chant for the hand of the upright man,
On the tower, like a spider,
A hand of copper,
Carefully moved,
So it sends a call in the dark:
"Prayer, prayer."

* * *

At the end of the frightful phantom procession,
A watchman saw two phantoms,
Walking, not knowing when that was or where.
The winds bite in their arms in the thick darkness.
Some life remained in the two phantoms,
But their eyes were closing,
And "prayer, prayer"
Chimes in their ears in the evening darkness.

* * *

"Don't you see?"

And no phantom remained on the road.

* * *

In the large Brahman temple,
Where deep ambiguity reigns,
Where Buddha's strangeness wraps the place,
Pray those whose eyes do not die,
Watched by that spider
On the tower, deep in silence.
The voice rises, large, of deep echo like Time,
And the two phantoms shiver.

* * *

"From the damp, cold castle
"From the darkness of houses,
"From the giant balconies,
"From the tower, where the spider's hand
"Points to us, in silence,
"From the roads, that chew the silent darkness,
"We came to you dragging our pale secrets,
"We came to you, we, the slaves of Time,
"Its captives, whose eyes do not die.
"We came to you dragging our shame,
"To ask your pardon, for these guilty eyes,
"In the depth of their depth, settled in the grief of years,
"And the voice of our tired conscience,
"Husky, of horrible ring.
"We came to you, who spray sleeplessness
"On the eyes of the guilty,
"On the eyes of the fugitives,
"To their past, to take refuge there, by a hill of ashes
"From the future of green eyes.
"O you whom we see day and night,
"Driving Time,
"Staring, whose eyes do not wink,
"His hands folded,
"On a thousand secrets.
"We came, sullying these foreheads
"On the floor of his temple, in submission.
"We call him without tears,
"And cry: Ah!
"We are tired, let us sleep,
"So that we cannot hear the voice,
"Calling to us: 'Prayer!'
"When the clock chimes two,
 "And the pallid guards do not knock
"On every door, with their outworn hands,
"Consumed by centuries,

"Leaving nothing of them but a heap of bones,
"We are tired. . . . Let us sleep,
"Sleep and forget the hand of the Spiderman,
"On the tower court scattering,
"Over the houses,
"The charms of their spiteful curse.
"Your mercy, Buddha,
"On the sleepless eyes,
"And let them finally die."

* * *

In the large Brahman temple,
The thrilling Buddha moved,
Stretching his arms to the two phantoms,
Blessing their tired heads,
Crying to the wretched guards
And to the man upright,
On the tower, in glory:
"Return them!"
                Then silence enwrapped the place,
And nothing was left except the night,
Buddha and the face of Time.

(*Complete Works*, vol. 2, 1971, pp. 391–399; orig. pub. 1949)

From *The Moon Tree*
(1968)

شجرة القمر

26. MY LOVE ROAD

My road to you passes by invisible valleys,
Absented by desires' fog and fragrance of yearning.
Upon the remote pinnacles, niggardly curtains drop,
Scraping away their areas' secrets, from the site of years.

* * *

My road to you, and what a strange, exciting road!
Villages draped by doubts, and dubious stretch of spaces,
Where doubts haunt, and a wondrous riddle reign.
On their heights my questions shout, but no answer is heard.

* * *

Many a vague town is there, and many arduous hamlets,
Where contradictions sleep, and in the valleys lie,
Where joy so sadly sighs, where song inspires
A long stillness and many forgotten memories.

* * *

Many deserts there are, where thirst lives in their sand,
I have relegated my tears, and for it, I
Have gathered dew, drop by drop, and on its arid land I poured
My blood;
              as my like on its like may die.

* * *

My love road is but vague uplands, and land of shade,
And wastes ever desiring, asking for the unattainable,
Where there are rivers of questions and impossibilities,
Where nights anchor for months, the moon forgets to run.

* * *

Between the two impossibilities: my arrival, then my return,
Pass winds, my tears made wet.
I stay awake, and labor, deep in grief and awe.
Perhaps I can open a road for my love among my ribs.   (1960)

(*Complete Works*, vol. 2, pp. 455–457)

27. BUSY IN MARCH

Roses sleep or wake,
And smiles, in the distance,
A fresh night or break of a morn.
The same is this or that,
My love, you are busy.
In vain are my chords,
Praying, and my chants.
On your cold desk you bend without dreams,
Your soul is stolen by figures.
At your locked door, the chants recoil.
I may laugh, or weep, and wake at night, or sleep,
The same it is, you are busy,
With your papers, and love on your desk is slain.
O, down with papers and pens!

* * *

Fresh March and I, behind the door,
Spray your serious forehead with fragrance,
We wave in the inkpot some of the waves' desires,
And save the desk wood from the cold and snow.
We present you with dew and fragrance in a cup to drink.
My dear, open the doors.
The affectionate moon, and I came knocking on the window.
We crossed the rocks and thorns,
And valleys of sighs and pains.
We came here to see you,
My love, so open the window.

* * *

Time passes and doors refuse us.
Oh, my tired, busy love,
Open, we are here.
The sun and myself
Came bearing the river tan,

With cups of perfume.
A bunch of stars and light,
My love, open the doors,
We are all here:
You, March, our love joy, and myself.

(*Complete Works*, vol. 2, 1971, pp. 474–476; orig. pub. 1963)

28. ICE AND FIRE

You ask what I mean? No, leave me, do not ask.
Do not knock on this door of this locked corner.
Leave me, a dropped curtain is hiding my secrets.
For behind the curtains, there are roses that may fade.

* * *

If I were to reveal, if I stripped my love-visions
And corners, laden with longing in my heart,
You would be angry with me, and would revolt against my sin,
And your reproach would grow thorns on my way.

* * *

And if you went on reproaching me, should I withdraw?
Can my flaming heart accept your reproach ice?
And I accept? No anger? No confusion?
No, I shall revolt against you. Anger will devour me.

* * *

If I revolted against you, and deranged the situation
By a rough word, or resentful letter,
You would be angry, rise in silence and aversion.
You would go, Adam, not asking about Eve.

* * *

But if you went, and left longing behind,
As a thirsty sparrow, not dreaming of water,
And nights that know neither dawn nor sunrise,
And if you went. . . . What would be left behind?

* * *

No, do not ask, let me be silent and withdrawn.
Leave my news and songs where they are,
Leave me to have questions and secluded answers
And roses that remain bent under your ice.

* * *

Adam, do not ask. Your Eve is folded
In a corner of your heart, perplexed and forgotten.
This is what was decided by destiny.
Adam is like ice, Eve is fiery.

(*Complete Works*, vol. 2, 1971, pp. 487–489)

29. A LOVE SONG FOR THE WORDS

Why do we fear the words?
While, sometimes, they are roses, palms
Of cool fragrance, that sweetly over cheeks passed,
Sometimes there are cups of refreshing nectar,
Sipped, one summer, by a thirsty lip.

* * *

Why do we fear the words?
Some of them are secret bells,
Whose echo announces, of our upset lifetime,
A period of enchanted dawn, generous,
Dripping feelings, love, and life.
So why do we fear the words?

* * *

We have resorted to stillness,
Keeping silent, not wishing the lips to reveal the secret.
And we thought there was a monster in the words we could not see,
Crouching, hidden by letters against the centuries' hearing.
We have fettered the thirsty letters,
Did not let them spread the night for us,
A support dripping music, fragrance, and hopes,
And warm cups.

* * *

Why do we fear the words?
They are a love backdoor, through which enters
Our vague tomorrow. So let us lift the silence veil off it.
It is a light window through which peep
What we have kept and covered in our depths
Of hopes and desires.
So when will boring silence discover
That we have come to love the words?

* * *

And why do we fear the words?
They are the friends that come to us,
From our very depth of warm and luscious letters.
They surprise us when our lips are inattentive,
They sing for us, then a thousand ideas rain on us,
Of fertile, and fresh horizons' life.
That settled in us when life was unaware.
Tomorrow, they will be dropped between our hands,
The friends who care about us: the words.
So why do we not like the words?

* * *

Why do we fear the words?
Some of them are fluffy sweet,
With letters that borrowed desires' warmth from lips.
Others are happy and jubilant,
That crossed, of rosy joys and drunken eyes,
Poetic, and fresh words,
Approaching to touch our cheeks,
Letters in whose echoes slept rich color and rustle,
Yearning, and hidden desires.

* * *

Why do we fear the words?
If their thorns had once wounded us, in the past,
They had rounded our necks with their arms,
And poured their sweet fragrance on our yearning.
If their letters have pricked us,
And turned their stalks away, and did not sympathize with us,
Many a promise they have kept in our hands,
And tomorrow they will lavish on us perfume, roses, and life.
Ah, fill our two cups with words.

* * *

Tomorrow we shall build a nest for us, of dreams of words,
Lofty, with ivy nesting on its letters.
We shall melt poetry in its decoration,
And will refresh its flowers with words,
We shall build a balcony for perfume and bashful rose,
With pillars of words,
And a cool passage, swimming in a thick shade,
Guarded by words.

* * *

Our sweet lifetime we have vowed as a prayer.
To whom shall we pray. Except to the words?   (1954)

(*Complete Works*, vol. 2, 1971, pp. 490–495)

30. DEO VOLENTE

One morning I called the rose and said: "Oh, rose, I am thirsty!"
It peeped, sprang, and smiled:
A face, a heart, a lip, and eyelashes.
It offered me perfume, color, love and was generous
As it spread out its cheeks and bent.

* * *

Then I asked my sweetheart to meet him.
He looked in my face and said yes, *Deo Volente!*
A couple of words, then he left,
A promise from him, and excitement from my heart, and contentment.
Tomorrow, or after tomorrow, he will come, *Deo Volente!*

* * *

Deo Volente!
A promise on the tulip lips, with fragrance covering the meadow,
A dawn light shining behind dazzled distances,
And breezes crossing over enchanted valleys.
Deo Volente! Overflowing visions of a song, dew, and prayer.
Deo Volente! Hymns and echoing bells,
Gaiety of a cup touching a cup.
Deo Volente! Outflow of celebrations and life,
A meeting of vineyards and water.

* * *

Deo Volente! And rich rains poured down,
Bursting the world with greenery.
Deo Volente! The sea surged and gave us
Fish, pearls, and spray refreshing our faces and visions.
Deo Volente! A thousand hands waved, a thousand chords woke,
A thousand moons glittered around me,
And I am still living and dreaming I shall meet him.
When will your dawn shine for me, O *Deo Volente?*

* * *

"When" and "will" are the tune of imploring eyelids and lips,
Their answer is *Deo Volente!*
Will you come to me? When the rain falls?
Will perfume be generous and pour?
Deo Volente!
        Deo Volente!
When will the sugar sap run,
Into the sour pomegranate? The dawn, when will it appear?
The shore, after the travel fatigue, when shall we see it?
Deo Volente?

(*Complete Works*, vol. 2, 1971, pp. 513–516)

31. A SONG OF SUMMER NIGHTS

O, confident quietude!
O jovial space of supple glitter,
Quaffing the stars as a cup of nectar.
O visions dripping color.

* * *

You are fragrance and softness,
Rustling, and slopes of rays,
And stars reflected in a deep brook,
And mellow chants.

* * *

You are a fountain of silence,
Fragrance, and coolness,
O pillow of distant jovial stars,
O home of yearning.

* * *

What coolness and softness,
O lips of lunar kisses,
Scattering dew as honey cups
Over the town trees.

* * *

What a river of perfumes,
In its fragrance: A swimming pool for the moon,
And nourishment for visions and conversation,
And a nectar for the feelings.

* * *

You are a home for the dreams,
O cool refuge of sweet neighborhood
For cheeks that bear the daily chores,
And come to you now, jovially.

* * *

Plunge me in shades,
And bear my soul on perfume breeze,
And grant my cheek a pillow near a star.
O nights, O nights!

* * *

If I drowse, then spread
Your refreshing cool and perfume as a bed
And melt the sweet moon into a brook,
And let your softness be my cradle.

* * *

And grant me a thousand dreams,
In nights of dusky shroud,
Which my joy drank to the lees.
Since they are my guitar and vine.

(*Complete Works*, vol. 2, 1971, pp. 530–534; orig. pub. 1952)

32. RIVER IN LOVE

"Composed during the horrible flood of 1954."

Where should we go?
It is running to us
Across the wheat fields, and not turning its steps,
Spreading its arms to us,
At the gleam of dawn,
Leaping, like the wind, jovial.
Its arms will meet us,
And fold our horror, wherever we go.

* * *

It is running and speeding.
It is silently pressing through our villages.
Its groundwater invades, checked by no dam.
It is desperately following us, to fold our youth
In its arms, to give us yearning to drink.

* * *

It is still following us with a smile of love.
Its wet feet
Have left their red marks everywhere.
It has played havoc east and west,
In yearning.

* * *

Where shall we run to?
It has rounded its arms,
On the shoulders of the town.
It works slowly, resolutely, and silently,
Pouring from its lips
Muddy kisses, covering our sad pastures.

* * *

That lover we have known for long,
It never stops its creeping toward our heights.
For it, we built and raised our villages.
It is our usual visitor, still generous,
Every year it comes down the valley,
And comes to meet us.

* * *

For it, we emptied our hearts under the night,
We shall accommodate it and leave,
It follows us in every land,
For it we pray,
For it we pour our complaint
Of the boring life.

* * *

It is now a god.
Have not our buildings on it washed their feet?
It rises and throws its treasure
Between their hands.
It offers mud, and death we cannot see.
Who do we have now, except it?

(*Complete Works*, vol. 2, 1971, pp. 535–538; orig. pub. 1954)

33. TO A WHITE ROSE

O treasure of coolness, nectar, and store of fragrant softness,
O light of a silken cheek, white, joy to the eye,
O white, home of butterflies of the expected spring,
The sun hopes you could give its light other gifts,
The dawn, your faithful follower, pauses your shade in the river,
O meeting point of love of brooks, larks, and trees,
O for the humans!
    They passed by your treasure, asking,
    Poor, what do you have?

* * *

O white, you and I will keep the exciting secret,
Your secret and mine we shall not divulge to the blind caravan.
What have we owned? No lands, no slaves, no palaces,
Nothing but the shiver of the moon, reflected in the brook,
And the song of the evening breeze, of fluffy passage,
The friendship of the sparrow, the colorful dawn and fragrance,
Love of the tender son, the kisses of the plentiful rain,
The soft pillow of grass.
O Mercy for the questioners,
And their question: What do you have?

(*Complete Works*, vol. 2, 1971, pp. 559–560; orig. pub. 1952)

34. TO POETRY

From the temple incense in age-old Babylon,
From the clatter of waterwheels in the southern lands,
From the cool wing of wakeful lark,
And the echo of the reapers singing the sunset tune,
That sound, your sound will return
To my life, to the hearing of years,
Laden with the perfume of a sad evening,
Which the cornstalks overfilled with elated fragrance,
With a strange, poetic echo,
Of the quack of a frog in the drowsy night,
Its monotonous, slackening sound
Fills the night and brooks.

* * *

That sound, your sound will return
To my life, to the hearing of the evening.
It will return; and in it I shall hear singing
Of lunar sweetness, with an echo of the rainy nights,
Of the tree branches' serenity,
When, drunken, it sips the sky nectar,
The nectar perfumed by the clouds,
And by the visions, by the greetings of the star.

* * *

I shall roam through the world
And shall gather the particles of your voice from every cool spring
In the northern mountains,
Where even tulips whisper songs,
Where the pine trees relate to the touring Time,
Stories pulsing with perfume,
Stories about the shade love of the brooks,
About the wolves' songs to the spring waters,
In the shade of the forest,
About the gravity of pastures

And the philosophy of the running brook,
About a lamb that is deeply depressed,
Spending the day grazing on grass and ideas,
Around in the fog of deep existence.

* * *

I shall gather the particles of your voice from the laughs of bliss
On an ancient evening
Of the Tigris evenings,
When the atmospheres were laden with longing.
From the gaiety of the revellers
Sipping the gargling waters
As they beat on their shore, and moonlight,
The summer moon, filling the evening atmosphere with images,
And the breeze passing like touching lips,
From another country,
A night of Scheherazade atmosphere
In its gentle night,
Everything is felt and dreamed, even silence,
And falls in love with light.

* * *

I shall hear your voice, wherever I may be,
In excited nature, in moments of madness,
When the echo of the thunders
Is laden with a thousand myths about the youth of existence,
About ages that vanished and nations that will never return,
About the stories of 'Ād boys to *Thamood* girls[1]
And stories sung by Scheherazade
To that mad king
In the winter nights.
I shall hear your voice every evening
When the light drowses,
And the troubles resort to dreams,
And ambition sleeps and sleep the hopes and love.
When life sleeps and Time remains

Awake and cannot sleep,
Like voice, filling the drowsy night,
Your wakeful voice,
In my deep yearning,
Your everlasting voice that does not sleep,
It remains with me, awake,
And I feel its color echo, filling every road
With perfume, with the dew of colors,
Your unknown voice.
I realized O, what joy, its honeyed secret.
I realized it, I alone, with the silence of Time.   (1950)

1.   *'Ād and Thamood were two extinct Arabian tribes.*

(*Complete Works*, vol. 2, 1971, pp. 561–566)

35. DISPUTE

The time of serenity is gone. It withered with memories.
And here we are in dispute,
Now came the time of struggle,
No gentleness, no smiles, no show of yearning.

* * *

And here we are in dispute, having buried harmony,
Behind the tension at the bottom of our tepid words,
Leaving no cup or spring for love,
Nor a nest for our sleepless dreams.

* * *

And here we are, revealing what was folded,
Of pretty flaws in our souls' depth,
And each realizes that love
Has folded what it could of our original, luxurious flaws,
Leaving nothing but our crude, impossible merits.

* * *

And here we are, knowing our distant limits,
What roughness extended in their depth,
How we acquired wonderful, varied flaws,
Hiding their faces behind a drape of contentment and ease,
Behind gentleness and peace.

* * *

In the moments of serenity, we touched our decent aroma
And tasted our generous, original merits,
And that varnish that wrapped our ambiguous depths
And covered our foolishness and weakness.

* * *

In the moments of yearning, we liked
Our simplicity and sweetness.

And here we are, in love with what humanhood creates in us.
We touch our awesomely wide depths,
And what lies in our foolishness of romantic beauty and fertility.

* * *

We had loved the burst of warmth in our eyes.
So let us now love depletion.
We had loved the blooming and poetry on our lips.
So why don't we now love pallor?
And why don't we leave a spot of hatred on our hands?

* * *

We had made friendship among our merits.
So let us now raise the foundations of love among the flaws
And allow a space for some follies and sins.
And let us be humans, overflowing with madness,
And leak some warm laughter and tears.   (1954)

(*Complete Works*, vol. 2, 1971, pp. 503–506)

From *The Sea Alters Its Colors*
(1974)

يُغَيِّرُأ لوانَه البحر

36. THE SUN MIRRORS

"'Abdulhādi, my husband, made me a gift of a Palestine map."
The original Arabic names of the Palestinian
towns and places are used here.

Sleep on, my eyelashes, O its map,
And flutter in my blood.
To break its fetters
I vowed my time, my blood, my song
Its horizons I shall mark with roses
I shall plant at the bleeding Bait Al-Maqdis[1]
A large carnation
And turn it across the sea,
An island of water lilies and oleander.
A tulip, warmly flourishing, I shall stick at Akka[2] frontiers.
Al-Ludd I shall gently grant
A red rose, nourished by the blood
Of an Arabian woman martyr.
Jenin I shall give dusk-colored fresh poppies.
For Ghazza I choose a fresh tulip.
For Kufre Qasim a thousand lilacs
That I shall scatter and twist into plaits.
On the approaches to Bisān
I shall plant a jasmine bush,
And violets near Haifa, Yaffa,
And the stabbed Nablus.
By Ṭolkarm, a narcissus
To awaken memories, sunny like mirrors.
My eyelashes are here, O its map,
So sleep on them,
As I am a prisoner of its widowed orange groves.
I arranged them with roses,
And they survived behind my excitement walls,
Lived their sad, beautiful towns

Until I planted my heart, with its dim candles,
A town on its map.

* * *

No, no; names of flowers, my hand!
Its bad I shall dot with my tears.
With tear drops, I shall draw the boundaries
Of my Nāṣira.
With sobs I shall build my Beer Sab.'
The Jaleel walls I should surround with luscious green,
Pouring from my pain and rejection.
I shall grant Laṭroon the tempest
Of my sorrows and surround them with my pulse.
The tawny baby Ramallah, I shall put to a cradle,
Cooled by the ice of tears.
And the sorrow around its rosy covers,
Our sails, roundelays, and candles.
I shall plant the melancholy heart a bush,
A moon illuminating all my land at night.
From north to south our villages soaked in my tears,
My sorrows roses cluster in their townships,
Perfuming every corner and side.
With my tears I marked the pavements in Al-Khaleel
And quaffed of my grief jars of nectar,
And had enough of wailing.

No, no, I am relieved of the tearful frontiers,
And I worried if my map should look at me
from these sorrowful towns.
I shall raise a revolt in their heights,
A rage, a smoke,
And at the pleading, black-eyed hamlets
I shall raise a festival of the shell blaze.
Death perfume will spread to intoxicate our enemies.
Neither will my fresh-colored roses heal the prick of memory,
Nor will my profuse warm tears.

I would rather surround these towns,
With daggers and swords
And keep them in a forest
Of sharp trees that would,
By stinging sharp knives,
By violence, wrench away the usurped meadows.
I should fly to stick a dagger at 'Akka gate
And build around Al-Quds pavements of thunderbolts
And plant the walls with thorns,
And around Tel Aviv to the ground.
I shall surround Ghazza with shells;
I shall sow around Yaffa minefields and fire.
At night I shall turn it into a field of fiery pomegranates.
I shall spread the peaceable downs,
With loving missiles and guns.
God is greater, O vineyards,
All arcades, O trees.
In you I shall sow my weapons
And wait for the harvest.
I should awaken your heights,
To the volcanoes of challenge and obstinacy,
I swear and refuse to wet my songs with tears.
I put my map between my hands,
I saw the heights of its towns turned waste
Of betrayed roads.
Their silence sown my nothing,
Inhabited by the air.
Their nights are nothing, their moans are withered,
Which suck me, push back my steps,
And keep me away from its thirsty plantations,
Turning my map into scattered rowing,
Its stones have no pulse, no veins, no blood;
Even my flame is extinguished.
I ploughed the rocks
But could not find any victory tulip,
My dawn's forehead was lost from me.

The fog approached, and pulled its blind down,
And covered my day, and I chewed my defeat thorns.

The town squares are muffled against me;
Their outskirts are difficult to reach.
What reaching?
The night separates us,
The flood sweeps us away,
Dreams drop dead, solutions fail,
Days betray me,
Through my fingers, even the seasons fall.
I felt I have moved far,
Far away and meeting was lost.
The hope clusters dried
And extended between me and its hills, the towns of weeping.
I learned that the secret of distance,
The secret of loss was that I have forgotten
To inscribe the name of God
On its rocks
And deprived them of its light and warmth.
Apologies to its soil, roses, and rivers.
I usurped the secret of its power.
Its lands accepted said poverty,
I offered it fatal aridity.
No, I shall return to my map,
And spread the Qur'ān's wings on every field
Until I see the name of God inscribed on its trees,
Kept the heart of its vineyards,
Sparkling in the rhythms of its songs,
Until I see the name of God,
Dews and greenness,
Fragrance and plenty,
In all its orange groves.

I shall break the fetters of my map
With all my weapons,

My roses, tears, the sharp knives,
And the name of my Lord
Will all open a fast road for me
So I find myself in my Palestine,
With stars filling my road,
With birthday candles,
And clarity behind my eyelashes
I move, liberating, in the name of my Lord,
And by my weapons, by roses and shining tears,
The towns of blood and wounds,
Until we can, she can, her dispersed people can
Embrace the morning,
And my beloved map returns
To my heart, under my eyelashes.
No one can tour its lower slopes
Except me,
Except the songs, Arab sentiment, and winds,
And feel my map fluttering as a star,
At the end of remote space,
And I grow a wing.

1. *Original Arabic name of Jerusalem.*
2. *Arabic name of Akre.*

(*The Sea Alters Its Colors*, 1974, pp. 412–418; orig. pub. January 27, 1974)

37. BIRTH OF THE VIOLET RIVER

My Monarch, upon my words plant me wings,
And sprinkle on my songs a morn,
And saddle the winds,
To sprinkle your tune on me, higher and higher,
And grant me what is sweeter,
A gleam of light from your forehead,
And let me see how under your eyes,
Grow new pastures,
And new puffs of perfume,
New forests of shade and love,
And lets me see how the poem shines up,
And how its baby steps begin.

My tune tries to pour between your hands,
My Monarch, and my lightning dims near you
Your regal face dazzles me
And stops my song in closure and stutter.
The reins of the poem drop out,
Its commas turn into circles.
The spiral rhymes escape,
And dry between my hands the ink pots
Its hemistitches flee to the long bypasses.
And the poem is lost.

The rhymes fly far and spread,
Across the night, their dishevelled hair.
They laugh at me, jump, refuse to come down,
Its sections dance across the distance,
An amazing dream.
The wind plucks cornstalks
From its eyelashes,
And below me flood their hemistitches,
As a brook,
It disappears when I touch it.

Its butterflies in my fingers calm down,
Its cornstalks freeze,
And I fail to catch the poem.
I tried to catch the hemistitch,
And hold a measure,
Then I recoil.
The rhymes escape me,
Naked, scattered.
I feel the night is tearing itself,
Grieved for me,
And that its stars are sobbing.
New sighs bite me.
Across the night I burn.
I wither with grief, I scatter,
And fail to gather the blossoms of the poem.
I remain scattered in the darkness and lost.
Your royal light distracts me, the sections digress,
I wonder, lost in the passes of the poem across the streets,
And sail on roads and fields.
Your face features are stamped by fog,
My soul stamped by tears,
Veiled by black scarves,
Between you and me the night falls
In a thousand curtains and doors,
And hides me from a thousand shelters.
The poem remains a city wall,
Muffled by sorrowful forts.
The poem remains questions and their echo,
Without an answer.
I whisper: "God is greater!"
The silence branch fructifies
And alters the night face.
A star rains
On my lips, a granary grows.
The face of the poem approaches,
Burning, swinging,

Ray by ray, refreshing my soul,
Getting all my wounds,
And plants me a rose,
Over my arid hill slopes.

So, is it like this?
When I whisper your name,
The store of fresh meanings opens,
The poem grows on my lips
Its slow steps
The rustle of distant winds.
My Monarch, you are the poem,
And you are the beauty.
From your face light
Rises the dawn of obstinate rhymes,
A unique person in the dark.
And the poem is born with me,
Like the birth of Venus
From the sea foam, floating like a rose.
Its plaits are floating hemi stitches,
Its eyelashes are letters and words.
For a pillow, the night offers its eyelashes, love and wake.
The sea foam offers its cheek,
Sparkling into its measures a dusk, snow, and butter,
Feeding them the glitter of pearls,
Forming the jewels into rhymes.
It scatters a rainbow and grows vineyards.
Pours the nights cold,
Its blue waves into two sections,
And sends my song
Of sweet ink and marine lips
Scented by orange fragrance.

And the poem is born with me,
Swings of vision, a new world.
God drips it, a twinkling star,

A violet river,
A vineyard canopy of his in blue feelings,
And dawns in the light, the dearest gift,
The sweetest,
The gentlest, the loveliest damsel.

(*The Sea Alters Its Colors*, 1974, pp. 419–424; orig. pub. March 5, 1974)

38. THE FIRE STALKS

"One winter, the fire fructified, so love flared in three circles,
the fire turned yellow, then red, then white,
burning the eyes of whoever gazed into it."

(1)

Dance in the winter stove, O fire!
The night eyelashes yield tears, the cold is biting,
On my soul below heedless gales,
In my heart sleeps a winter,
On my wakeful eyelash branches fall rains,
The hurricane slashes my thought
And knock, on my memory door,
Eyes, faces, news,
From the past and knock me down.
Humid cares of icy drapes
Mountains of thoughts and seas turn me over.
The fire creeps and burns my blood snow.
Its heat touches my tune.
Its flame pours summer on my lute
And wakens the chords' sleep.
The fire wind carries me
To all love circles,
The three of them, and grows on my heart
Two wings of dream and memory.
Without the fire, there would not have been fruits of love,
I knew the flare of feelings around its flame,
As my feelings are depths,
Their mythical passes are my loss,
Which leads me to a lost, foggy world.
It has pillars, vaults, walls.
From the fires begin my trip,
My roads open for me,
And the trips my soul will snatch.

In my elated branches, the fire sap may run,
The love roses and poems,
It is the fruits.
And every love I feel,
Oh night, is a circle,
A color in the fire flame.
Its reality is reflected to me,
By the fire mirrors.
My first felt love, my small circle,
Is loving one of the people,
Air, a star on my forehead,
In my hair a band of myrtle.
His smile is fields of fragrance,
A tune of bells.
It sweetens me, decorates me, crowns me
On the kingdom of illusion
And in the courts of dream. . . . A princess.
It turns me younger and changes me
Into colorful lips, a skirt, and a braid.
His love is a summer of roses, singing in my blood,
His face is a sparrow wandering across my sky,
His name is a cornstalk on my lips.
It gave me wings and opened my heart as windows of light
And turned my life into a rich, green field.
It made my song a water lily,
And cast all-night stars into my cup
The fire flames humanized the person of my love for me,
They wrote out his face for me from the dusk of memory,
As a sky in the garbs of sunset.
His face, a red rose or a glare,
My heart, or a bird's wings floating in the southern wind?

His face, or the fire rose and a cluster of sparks?
Intonations of earthly love in my soul of a line of images?
Seas in my blood or sails?
Roundelays and full waves of yearning,

Of love and other passions?
Memories of meetings in my eyes?
Or exaggerations of wakeful hours?
Sparks of flames or a field
A smiling face or rain scent?
Or evening walks in seasons?

Passions turned me around, O fire!
I am a yellow rose in the meadow,
Flared by storms and weather change,
Cast on rocks that tear it
And burn it
And give her the feeling that it enjoys, shade and water,
And give perfume in a world of fragrance.
The fire stove changed,
With the feeling in my heart,
The fire stove changed,
Its fire turned yellow,
The color of doubt, passions, and jealousy.
The color of my yearning and errant thoughts,
With all that is in love, desire, silence, and confusion,
Vibrating like a straw in the lap of a storm,
Lost in the dangerous love valleys,
I put on the fire coat,
My song loses its way in the night,
Swayed by love and torrents.
She may fall in a wave of thoughts,
A look may capture her,
Like love in this fire, evading flames that cannot be touched,
Clouds of liquid flame, a desire boat of yellow mast,
A river of revolting waves, mad, cannot be contained.
A boisterous tempest, and a saw's incision,
My fire, O my fire,
My earthly, uncontrolled love is like your yellow face.
Touching both is warmth,
The tastes of both are sugar,
Their kisses wound like a dagger.

(2)

My fire in the wave of this yellow stove,
Oh, my fire, melt me,
Cleanse and lift me,
In my earthly love I have spent my years,
To the second, middle circle, take me,
And resurrect me,
In the night, a lisping lark, yearning for the groves of Yaffa and Jenin.

Love of the land is purer
Than love that allowed my feeling,
And sprayed, with mud- passions and fever my forehead.
Love of the earth's forests, bricks, and wheat.
Its love is a marble balcony.
Its love washes my doubt in lakes of certitude,
Its love plans me as an azure boat,
Swimming in a river of paradise.
The love of land is music and tenderness,
A river of rhythm and bells of yearning,
In its meadow I am a sparrow of a grain store,
A handful of its sand is a dawn star,
A dream,
A basket of amber.
Its echo reverberates,
In my prayers, song and silence,
In my yearning supplication.

Its visions find a cover
Among my eyelashes,
Memories and roundelays, a history of cool green shade,
I remember, I remember,
All the centuries' glories,
All my olives, my dear ones' groves, my clay,
Every field in its land,
Once gave faces, promises, and fluctuated.
Every perfume and breeze filling and intoxicating the meadow,

Every star in its remote high horizon came down,
To attend the feast and revel.

In the love of Palestine, I live two lifetimes,
And swim in two circuits,
The fairies of two seas for me dance.

My love for her changes the essence of fire,
The fire stove altered,
The yellow flame turned into bright red embers,
With a size, form, and idea behind its blaze
If I wanted to touch it with my hands,
To distribute it here and there, and scatter it, gather it,
Then spread,
One brand here,
One brand there,
One brand there,
Our eyelashes suck its warmth,
And take it to answer my yearning blood,
And my poems' warmth,
My candles, my hymns, and roaming,
The redness of those brands,
Is blood running,
In the color of anger bleeding from Palestine wounds,
The redness of those brands,
Is blood-red roses from Deir Yaseen gardens,
Whose fragrance is soaked in a stabbed wound,
The redness of that brand,
Is like our plains of bloody waist,
Like our fields of disheveled hair,
Waterford by the martyrs' blood on a trip of resolve
To the valleys of revenge,
To the valleys of revenge,
To a future that opens for the home
Windows that overlook an expanse of moon meadows
And smashes the thorns of shame.

(3)

O fire! Destroy me,
Then forge me into another being, and build my forehead,
And from light letter fill my lips and eyes.
Wash and cleanse me,
Carry me across dark spaces,
To my upper that circle take me.
By fire high-rise to the apex of my longing,
I reject my suspicion and temptation,
To the sun, to the highest pinnacles,
My trunk and branches reach,
Where in the extent I meet my Monarch.

Like the white snow,
Like stars,
I meet my Monarch.
On my way He scatters love and chandeliers,
Endless shores, suns He casts for me,
And galaxies of light,
Rivers of sweet warmth, purified and refined,
In new movable skies,
Valleys of color and rose
Where, in their gardens, I am entertained,
Given to drink, and drink,
Cups and cups of nectar of summer stars.

His love, my Monarch's love, is a journey with no end;
His face contains the universe.
From his horizons begins every being.
His love is a doze, a lisping lark, a banner.
His love is my moon, a dewy lilac, a sky.
Canopies, vineyards, chords, and water.
His love is a meadow green, spreading across words and skies.
There horizon edges are a wonderful work of art.
The sound of their rustle is perfume and holiness.

Of their attraction I swim in a feast of colors.
The love of my beloved Monarch has changed the fire essence.
My stove altered, its flame filled in flower perfume,
In its purity melted secrets of the unknown.
Its fire became like lightning white.
Whoever casts a look at it
Will, unfortunately, dim his sight.
His eyelids will burn and smoke.
A whiteness of dazzling waves, no eyes could stand its morning glow.
A lightning that stuns man,
The light that violates the eyes inflames them,
Leaving them no vision, giving the soul what it gives:
Ray of light, a brilliant stretch of colors, is fire.
Eternity dozed in its waves, and Time slept.
Its fingers are touching me,
Dropping off my back the heavy slavery chains.
The fire whiteness dazzles me,
Enslaves me,
So I exit my being and my Time is folded.
I ascend with no bond to check me.
I rise in the heights, without my body.
Here is my home.
Here is my home.
My Monarch's love gathers all my scattering,
Collecting and raising me
To a dearer,
To a sweeter state,
To a higher state behind the reach of fire flame.
I swoon, I swoon, I cannot see even the fire.
I cannot remember even the poems.
I weighed in eight-day lightning,
And falls around my conscience and feeling a screen of whiteness.
I lose my words, myself, my feeling,
Across a forest of moons,
And die down, I cannot see,
It folds, dwindles, disappears the fire.   (September 1974)

(*The Sea Alters Its Colors*, 1974, pp. 425–437)

39. IMAGES AND DOZES

Before traffic lights

(1)

The green light comes on.
The dream smashed
And scattered.

O red! O sigh of a summertime rose,
Shimmering under polar snowstorms,
Over flame jutting out of gulfs,
Burning behind memory, in a whirlpool of colors,
In a forgotten world.
O dusk of red, stolen from the cheeks of a hungry boy,
O henna dye in a wild hand palm.
O arrow, stabbing through,
Across the African land.
The twigs of its vineyards are for crosses.
O greedy, that snatched the cup of pure water
From the thirsty lip.
The red came on! A wall rose behind the two hearts.
The stage curtain dropped.
They separated,
Dug two wounds,
With tears they washed two songs,
And cut two chords.

Red! Oh perdition, hidden in a July hurricane,
That handed the rose over to the eastern storming wind,
Violated the two rivers' sails,
And sucked up the lips' coral.
O full stop at the end of April words,
Stopping what we wish to hear after,
Does not give us perfume but distresses us with the ruins of the rose.
It plucks the rose from our souls' burning,

Exiles it from the foggy memory forests.
The rose falls and burns.
O red! O avid flame that burned the lark's throat,
Burned the lips of the singer at dawn,
And clipped the song's wings.

O lip crying, "No!"
Which nailed the passer over the hill, and broke the hope
Piece by piece. O bloody spray of negation!
O flower killer, O thorn on land ways,
O summer that departed,
Dragging the remains of its youth under October storms.
O mind of dusky idea, housing paralysis,
Which spoiled mythical waves and fields.
It effaced El Dorado and its golden uplands.
Out of my sight it folded them in a secret land.
It housed them in Saturn.
Happy is he who can reach them.

(2)

The yellow light came on.
The thin thread between dawn and the departing night darkness.
The first sparrow twitter,
Over the soft grass dreaming, spreading unknown fragrance,
Carried over the wet breezes of dancing hair locks.
It invades mountains and plains,
Love is God and revels,
Gives out intoxication to lovers,
With sweet pining and stupor.
On the poets' nests it sprays amber,
And porous jars of honey, to water wastes and fields.

The yellow light came on.
Color of blond cornstalks, growing in the lap of granary.
O silence between two lovers!

O silent desires settling in the eyes!
O yellow, color of marble!
The laughing meadow exclaimed in elation,
The cloudy forehead rained.
O crossroads!
O valleys pouring burning dusk, between two skies.
O introduction to realize a silver dream!
O dream of green gardens,
O memory of silver water springs.
O yellow rose in a forest of sadness and fog!
O dreamy lily sleep on book pages!
O moment of silence in a song!
O space of blaming and approach
Between two lovers who disputed for decades and decades.
O the good news of the wounded, coming out of the pit.
O moon entering from a skylight,
In case soldier's cell lost doors.
O sweet scent of rain,
Falling on dust and soil.
O nursery of blond roses, and vineyard scent.

The yellow light came on,
Our favorite passage, our blond valley.
Between the silence and the tune,
A space of secrets and revelation, between light and darkness,
In a lover's night, who lost his way, in a forest smile.

O clipped branch that bore fruit,
O labyrinth that turned fertile and moonlit in darkness.
O the pining of lover, dreaming in the dark,
And fields the curtained night, channels of paradise river,
And pillars of marble town.
O my yellow light, O the breezes' kiss
On the sleepless cheeks, all my tulip.
O stars necklace, O amber canopy,
Our night's end, O last star.

(3)

The green light came on.
The dream pointed to us, to take us to the land of sugar.
O my green light, my quest, my wake!
O my Monarch's face in the distance!
By his eyes' glare the lute chords break up in passion.
Death is mixed with birth.
For the joy of meeting, the moon's face cracks.
Turn away, darkness, and be buried.
So thousands of islands will twinkle,
Shores and uplands will dance,
The stunned times will collapse, spreading as feasts.
Feasts, feasts, feasts.
O my sweetheart's face in the distance!

O my green light, O drunk meadow,
On poured radiance!
O warm drop of passion in the bottom of the cup.
The color of the past was surrounded by memory,
Enthralled dewy horizons, dreaming passions, moons,
Fields of blond cornstalks in the lap of steppes.
The smile is born enthralled, on the sweetheart's face,
With love poems and rivers of milk and spice,
Songs we shall sing, swaying sails, and sunset,
Spices, perfumes, secrets,
Arabian future, from which poems are scooped up,
Bursting from the groves of the usurped homeland.
May its memory be greeted, by rain.
My sweetheart's face
Sweetly shines, from the fresh memory balconies,
From island shores, forged of silver.
And my sweetheart's name
Has letters, graced by rains,
Followed by deserts and seas.
O my green light!

O taste of morning in Makkah, dewy and perfumed.
O name of God intoned at night by chords,
And sung by the dazzled wind and fire.
Whoever tastes its sweetness gets drunk,
Revels, revels.

O my green light, O flame,
O my memory street, where the proud square raises
A statue for my sweetheart's name.
The ivy creeps over its letters,
And waves on its canopy perfume and fog,
And gold mixes with it.
Red rose bursts from its letters in sunset color.
The cane gives it the sugar,
Breezes undulate in my sweetheart's name,
And clouds refresh, with purity and pallor, roses,
Dancing, shaking their tenderness secrets, filling my sweetheart's
    name.
O my green light, O grapes,
Drip and rain,
Collect flowers,
Gather images,
For my sweetheart's name letters,
Pluck cherries from it and reap memories.

(4)

Among the red, yellow, and green,
You laugh, my heart, you weep, remember.

You walk and walk, where to?
The trip and darkness extend,
The desired land,
The meadows of pistachio and amber,
The Paradise rivers,
Behind the sea fog, are far.

My future is blocked roads.
My valleys are empty, when the wind whistles,
And a wounded secret starts to mumble.

My mountains are daggers,
My meadows are poems, weeping in the silent notebook.
My heart is beaten by chords, with keys digging into it.
O my warmth, my enchanted rain,
O canopies of crystal,
O my sweetheart's face,
O my sweetheart's face.   (January 11, 1974)

(*The Sea Alters Its Colors*, 1974, pp. 455–466)

40. SKY OVER THE CACTUS FOREST

Love and torture approached,
Enthralled, they smiled and melted bashfully,
Hand in hand,
Cheek to cheek.
Love and torture have in my heart's court settled.
Two children, coming from eternal nowhere.
In the morning, they distribute tears and kisses.
Their eyelashes are past and future,
A wave perfume and a flow.

Love said to me: "Good morning."
I said to love: "My morning is songs.
Two riverbanks,
Sky, birds!"
Sad torment said to me: "Good evening."
I said to torment: "My heart is departed skylarks.
And raining songs,
A forest inhabited by algae and cactus."

Love and torment said to me: "Take us, we are twins.
Two lost wounds,
Or two violin chords.
So dress us with songs, cover us with kisses.
And lodge us in the lost eternity in the eyes of silence."
Love and torment said to me:
"Love us, we are here two sparrows
In the forest of light and sorrows.
We are two sails of a lost barque,
And we are the birth and remains of life.
Fresh hope on our hands is coffins.
Sorrow is apples and two honey jars.
Poetry on our lips is two rivers,
Angelic sweetness with us, and the devil's savagery.
We are a grave and a morn, elegies and love songs.

Our face is July once,
And once April." Love and torment are two jailers.
Their prison around me is two paradises.
My chains are bracelets and a red rose band.
My prison door is a balcony overlooking worlds on ages.
Love and torment are rain fragrance.
Of their aroma the place is drunk.
Love and torment are modulation, and sea waves,
And oak shade,
A smile in sad eyes, two holy verses.
Love and torment are two windows
And orchard greeneries.

Love and torment are waves and two boats,
In a distant river with no banks.
They are my dates, my birth, and my second lifetime,
My days' perfume, my festival.
Their two sweet faces took me
To the land of poetry and song.
Love and torment have dispersed me.
In the windy roads they lodged me.
In the ways moans and tears they lost me,
To sadness they handed me over,
To damp songs of naked walls,
In its letters winter resides,
With boisterous winds and gales.
Love and torment are two notebooks.
In their silence I draw my sorrows.
Love and torment
Are a prison cell, with no door,
Two book pages
Effaced.
Love and torment are two tears,
Two roses.

Love and torment have sold me,
And my lute bought me.
It distilled me as an infatuation poem.
It made me a moment in song lifetime.
It anchored me as a wounded planet,
And burned me into intonation
And a chandelier's wound.
Oh, his face!
Oh, my trip!
Oh, road darkness,
Oh, star over my forehead,
Oh, sail of my drowned eyelid,
Oh, wound dusk, Oh, lightning fog.
My guardian angel? Or my devil?
Oh his distant face, and enemy are you or a friend?
You flourish in my being,
As death, a river of sunny nectar.
Oh, my dusk, Oh, taste of time.
Oh, my leafy wound.
Save you! O hermitage of songs.   (March 2, 1974)

(*The Sea Alters Its Colors*, 1974, pp. 438–442)

41. FOR US REMAINS THE SEA

We stood by the sea, under the midday sun, two excited children,
My soul swimming across your meadows,
In a river of two generous eyes.
My heart running, after a question
Of buds, carrying a pasture aroma on your lips.

Your question has the sweetness of the northern wind,
The splendor of a song poured by longing violins,
Hidden in your hands.
Your question is the color of the sky,
Over ponds and vineyards.
You asked if the sea alters its colors,
Do its waves change colors?
Do its shores alter?

You ask, and your eyes were as wide as visions.
Your face, a star gone far,
Lost ships that could not find a haven.
You ask, and your eyelashes were a child's surprise,
A cornstalk's quiver, a modulating field.
Your hands were two sails,
Dropping on two boats,
Wandering behind range and visions.
I said: Yes, my sweetheart.
The sea alters its colors.
Green ships sail across it.
Blond towns emerge from it.
It sometimes drinks the sunset's blood.
It sometimes assumes the color of space
And gathers its blueness, my love,
And dreams, gazing with azure eyes,
Sky colored,
To the endless, assuming the color of light
In the morning and turns all its chandeliers in the evening.

You asked about the sea: Does it change colors?
Do its waves alter in colors?
Do its shores alter?
Yes, my love.
The sea that beats my soul's valleys
And departs across heavens of color and sun
Across sunset fields.
The lunar dusk bathes in its waves, and wets its hair,
Casting to it a sky and an idea.
Yes, my love, yet, and colors its gulfs.
Yes, and alters colors,
Drinks the yellowness of my doubt and suspicion,
Becomes blue, like my tune color,
And sails, in its waves' azure, my songs and ships.
It becomes white, its wave turns a jasmine.
It becomes green, like the sad eyes green,
Like the aquamarine of Nahawand River,
In the bottom of my grief.

You asked about the sea: Does it change colors?
Your eyes were spacious seas,
Of lost limits and shores.
Yes, my love, it alters colors,
And takes the tint of ashes.
It has a taste of all sleepless nights.
Gray are all its fishes, and ash color
Are its pearls, sponges, and octopuses; and ash color
Are its towns of drowned domes,
And ash color is the forehead,
Of a floating drowned creature.
The salt cushioned its waves
In a swoon, swallowing water and salt,
With thorns and ashes on his lips.
My sea, and yours, is a sea of ashes,
The heart's yearning
Has cruelty that kisses the wound, spreads a soft pillow.

My sea and yours wrangled, with the grey, drowned body,
Sent its cruel wave to smite him,
The sea fairies to carry him,
To the forgetful russet sands,
To lie unconscious on the shore.
The sea of ashes
Sprinkles on his unconsciousness.
The drowned youth is courted, in the cheeks, by a wave of love,
Washing his forehead, and pouring
On him love, salt, and foam.
Once it covers the body,
And once it returns, recording,
And leaving him to eternal daze.

O you who asked me:
"Does my sea, and yours, alter colors?
And like clouds, colors, and paints its banks
In oil or coal?

My love, in my childhood I had a grandfather,
Tall, like the hair plaits of a leafy spring.
My grandfather had a depth,
A shade, a distance.
He had violence, like an autumn storm.
He had a space in unlimited, mysterious seas.
My grandfather was strong, like a fearful sea wave.

One day, fire flames ran into our house,
Starting by chewing the door, burning the tender drapes.
The flames ran in circles,
Roaring in our hope balconies, laughing at our horror,
Threatening to expand, running in our residential area,
Warning that it would consume cheeks,
Lips, and plaits,
That it would assassinate even granary youth.
My grandfather rushed like a sea wave,

Sending a shout of horror and fear,
Coming down like a blizzard, swearing and cursing.
His curses were rain and compassion.
His savagery, a tuned verse of poetry,
A prayer whisper, a dawn star,
A perfume-boat.
The stretch of swearing, on his lips, is a colored brook.
My grandfather extinguished the fire.
And saved my eyelashes and hair.

My love, and my grandfather was a sea!
He alters his colors. His eyelids turn black and green.
He changes his waves, expands, forms pearls.
He flows in springs, anchors on shores,
Creates an ebb, causes a flow.
He scatters blond islands across the blue gulf.
His cursing buckets were balm jars,
Breaking the fire bracelets by a subtle forearm and wrist.
The force of my sea waves, and yours, became hard palms and
    chest,
To carry the gray, drowned body, cover it with a rain of kisses
    and love,
And place it on the banks of peace,
Flutter of a pigeon wing,
To give it a new lifetime,
Plant dreams in the swoon,
With memory cornstalks, a cooling cloud.

About color and sea, you ask me, my love?
When you are my sail,
My sea colors,
The daze of the dream in my eyes.
You are my road fog,
You are my sails,
And you are my wave apex,
My sorrow rose, my pallor fragrance.

About the color, and sea, you ask me, my love?
When you are my seas,
My choral and shell.
Your face is my home,
So take my boat on a wrapped and hidden wave of yearning,
To a vague impossible shore,
With no planes or uplands,
To a dusk of lunar orbit, and deep nadir,
With no color at midday,
No part in thickness,
No horror, no peace.

There, we shall be lost,
Eat the winter warmth, and pluck spring snow,
And yarn the frost wool.

There, there is no length in our dream-shade, no shortness,
No record of destiny,
Nothing that sight could climb,
Except a song-wave, coming down the moon mountains.
We laugh, weep, and your eyes reflect the sea color.
And for us remain the color,
The sea,
And the expected eternity.   (June 5, 1974)

(*The Sea Alters Its Colors*, 1974, pp. 365–373)

NĀZIK AL-MALĀ'IKA

(1923–2007)

was an Iraqi poet and is considered by many to be
one of the most influential contemporary Iraqi female poets.
She taught at a number of schools and universities,
most notably at the University of Baṣrah and Kuwait University.

'ABDULWĀḤID LU'LU'A

is professor emeritus of English literature at Philadelphia University
in Amman, Jordan, and the author and translator of sixty-five books,
including selections from Samīḥ al-Qāsim, 'Abdulrazzāq
'Abdulwāḥid, Muẓaffar al-Nawwāb, and Badre Shākir Al-Sayyāb.